THE HOLY DOCTRINE OF LUCIFER

By

Dr. Amschel (pseudonym)

Contents:

"I had during many years followed the Golden Rule, namely, that whenever a published fact, a new observation or thought came across me, which was opposed to my general results, to make a memorandum of it without fail and at once; for I had found by experience that such (contrary and thus unwelcome) facts and thoughts were far more apt to escape from memory than favorable ones."

Charles Darwin. The Life of Charles Darwin, by Francis Darwin

THE FALL OF LUCIFER

Since the beginning of humankind, the concept of a battle between good and evil has been part of mythology, philosophy, and society. Many scholars argued the question about the creation of evil. The question is simple in its nature did God created evil or did man. Maybe because good exists there could be his absence or antithesis of good or evil (e.g. greed, lust, avarice, deception, sinning). The term Satan originates from the Hebrew, "the accuser", or in Arabic Shaytan, "the adversary". In a sense, if there is conceptual good, there could be the complete opposite. The Devil is the one who personalize evil, as a concept, he is the great enemy of good and civilization in general.

We live in an age of extraordinary social and technological advancement. Universal human rights, unprecedented medical innovation, complex global interconnections, and a whole new digital world have literally transformed our experience of the human world. We might even be at the apex of a civilized society. But within all of this progress, we have been unable to rid of one historical constant and we still live under its shadow... Evil still exists, and its definition still eludes (T. Clark, 2016).

The idea of the Devil, or evil incarnate, is like Good, a system. It is at once a part of human tradition and culture and provides a way to explain certain events, as well as allow temptation. Evil is a distortion in moral and philosophical thought, something as tangible as the deeds of the Nazi party, or simply a way to explain further genocide and the way humans can even conceive something so vast and horrible that the only possible way it could exist within the human psyche is for some outside force to hold control (Muchembled, 2003).

It always surprised me how many people are referring to Satan as Lucifer when actually the true meaning of the later is the planet, Venus. The term Lucifer was first used in King James Bible to refer to the morning star, with no relation to the Devil (Satan).

According to the Christian Bible, book Revelation 22:16: I Jesus have sent mine angel to testify unto things in the churches. I am the root and the offspring of David, and the bright and morning star.

It seems both of these terms Jesus and Lucifer are same, the morning star or otherwise known as planet Venus. The usage of the term morning star is all throughout the New Testament in reference to Jesus the Christ.

If we want to find out more about the origin of Lucifer, we need to look into the Old Testament, where the name "Satan" is mentioned 66 times, the "Devil" in comparison 34 times, but the name of "Lucifer" is cited only once.

The important note here is that while Satan quotations are all throughout the Bible, Lucifer quotation is only once, in Isaiah 14:12:

How art thou fallen from heaven, O Lucifer, son of the morning! How art thou cut down to the ground, which did weaken the nations! (King James edition) The translators of King James Version of the Bible, one of the chiefs of whom was the well-known Rosicrucian Dr. Robert Fludd, a fact which will no doubt shock and horrify many Christians, chose to translate this word with the Latin word "Lucifer." And in many translations, Lucifer is not even mentioned here:

How you have fallen from heaven, O morning star, son of the dawn! You have been cast down to the earth, you who once laid low the nations! (New International Version)

"How you are fallen from heaven, O Day Star, son of Dawn! How you are cut down to the ground, you who laid the nations low! You said in your heart, 'I will ascend to heaven; I will raise my throne above the stars of God; I will sit on the mount of assembly on the heights of Zaphon; I will ascend to the tops of the clouds, I will make myself like the Most High'" (Old Testament passage Isaiah 14:12-14). This identification, referring to Lucifer as a translation of the "morning star" or "bright star" alternatively "star of the morning" in principality refers to the Babylon king who was enemy in a war of the Israelites. The king is in his pride, glory, and fall. If one reads carefully it is obvious that the true power behind the Babylon king is the son of the morning, Lucifer.

The original Hebrew text uses the word which literally means "bright star" or "shining one," a term applied sarcastically or mockingly by the Israelites to this particular enemy of theirs. "Lucifer" literally means Light-bringer, Light-bearer, Bringer of Dawn, Shining One, or Morning Star. The word has no other meaning. Historically and astronomically, the term "Morning Star" has always been applied to the planet Venus.

Since the only occurrence of the word "Lucifer" in the Bible is that one verse in Isaiah, there is absolutely nothing in the Bible which says that Lucifer is Satan or the devil. It was Pope Gregory the Great (540-604 AD) who was the first person to apply that passage of scripture to Satan and thus to equate Lucifer with Satan. But even then this notion didn't catch on in a big way until the much more recent popularisation of John Milton's "Paradise Lost" in which Lucifer is just another name for Satan, the evil adversary of God. Also, such luminaries of the Christian world as Martin Luther and John Calvin considered it "a gross error" to apply Isaiah 14:12 to the devil, "for the context plainly shows these statements are in reference to the king of the Babylonians."

Thus the Christians who claim that Lucifer is the devil actually have no Biblical basis or authority for such a belief.

The concept of Lucifer, as the antithesis of God the creator, originates in early Christianity. The illiterate and erogenous assumption that Lucifer equals Satan "has battered its roots too deep in believers blind faith". It is necessary to allow the public to courageously, boldly, and freely discover the true origin and true essence of what Lucifer actually is.

He has become a "branded name," one which instantly braces up the image of the evil personified even in the minds of the unfaithful.

However, no one can deny that even Jesus is boldly proclaiming his identity related to Venus the Light bringer in Revelation 22:16, where he says "I, Jesus, am the bright and morning star." If the translators had chosen to translate this verse using Latin translation just as they did with Isaiah 14:12, it would read "I,

Jesus, am Lucifer."

Lucifer as the epitome of evil, however, needs not to be accepted as something mentioned in a book equal to the absolute truth.

"There is no religion higher than truth" – and sooner or later, the truth will succeed.

"Fīat jūstitia ruat cælum" is a Latin legal phrase, meaning "Let justice be done though the heavens fall." The ancient metaphor signifies the belief that there will be justice regardless of consequences.

The bringer of light, the divine spark of our souls or the name 'Lucifer'" has already been so totally 'Satanized' and identified with the devil, that saving it from that malevolent decayed image is a challenging undertaking.

Apparently, Lucifer's fall began when he becomes fascinated with his own good looks, refinement, potential, intelligence, and power leading him to want to acquire for himself the place belonging only to God. Lucifer's self-generated pride preceded the fall of the human Adam and it represents the origin of sin in the universe. Lucifer's personal choice to rebel against God originated from his right of "Free Will".

Furthermore, the "Book of Job" indicates: "Now there was a day when the sons of God came to present themselves before the Lord, and Satan also came among them" (Job 1:6).

Interestingly, here Satan is the son of God, and Lucifer is the son of God as well since God himself created Lucifer. "I form the light, and created darkness, I make peace, and created evil, I the Lord do all these things" (Isaiah 45:7).

Satan's well-known statement, where he is referring to God is: "I will assent above the heights of clouds, I will like the most high" (Isaiah 14:14). Obviously, Satan was hungry for glory, in love with his splendor, ambitious, if you ask him, he was king of kings, for him the only way was up.

Qur'an calls Satan "arrogant" for refusing to bow before Adam.

Archangel Lucifer is mistakenly brought into relation to Satan, which is a completely separate entity. Lucifer is angelic being characterized by his free will, pride, and power.

Many people believe they can gain significant spiritual power by invoking Lucifer and the angelic entities obeying him.

Ultimately, Lucifer does not exist to deceive people, but for people to learn from his story and his original sin-Pride.

PRIDE THE ULTIMATE SIN

Obviously, Bible views pride as one of the seven deadly sins sitting among terrible attributes like envy, greed and arrogance. In fact, it was Dante Alighieri who said that pride was the deadliest of the deadly sins.

Nonetheless, Lucifer original sin, pride is a positive emotion and healthy trait. The famous Greek philosopher Aristotle described pride with the phrase "crown of the virtues". It's an emotion we experience when we've accomplished something special, or someone who is close to us has.

Pride generally gets a bad reputation, but of course it helps to feel distinguished and self-aware of our personal worth. Proud people never allow others to walk all over them, but sometimes they may seem arrogant and narcissistic.

Much of the research in this area has focused on determining whether pride is good or bad for us. A solution has been to split it into two emotions: hubristic pride and authentic pride. Some researchers argue that hubristic pride is what leads to states of arrogance and smugness, while authentic pride is what promotes confidence and fulfilment (N. Mclatchie, 2017).

Specifically, authentic or beta, pride (I'm proud of what I did) might result from attributions to internal, unstable, controllable causes (I won because I practiced), whereas pride in the universal self (I'm proud of who I am), referred to as hubristic, or alpha, pride (M. Lewis, 2000; Tangney et al., 1989), might result from attributions to internal, stable, uncontrollable causes (I won because I am always winning).

Pride is positively related to self-worth, self-motivation, self-confidence, self-respect and personal acceptance.

Pride refers to feelings "generated by appraisals that one is responsible for a socially valued outcome or for being a socially valued person." (Mascolo, M. F.,& Fischer, K. W. (1995).

This definition, explains that a person is accountable for valued social outcome. Anyone would feel proud for their personal accomplishment.

Monett wrote, "I tell myself that anyone who says he has finished a canvas is terribly arrogant. Finished means complete, perfect, and I toil away without making any progress, searching, fumbling around, without achieving anything much." (House, J. (1986).

Frank Lloyd Wright said that early in life, having been given the choice between hypocritical humility and honest arrogance, he would chose the latter.

Recent studies concluded that pride is a universal signal of status. When one acts with pride, other people see him as possessing higher social status. Thus pride, sends a powerful signal to others. As already mentioned there are two types of pride: "Authentic Pride" and "Hubristic Pride." Both types of pride make person seem like possessing higher status and get him the respect but these two prides present with very different characteristics and come from very different psychological places. Authentic pride is satisfaction of the person who has accomplished a goal with his own effort. Hubristic pride is when person feels he is superior to everyone else.

High self-esteem individual's pride results from "attributions to internal, unstable, controllable causes (I won because I practiced)," (Tracy, J. L. & Robins, R. W. (2007)). In general, people of high-status "are likely motivated by pride on an almost daily basis are precisely the people whose prejudice could do the most harm, leading them to hire and fire others in a discriminatory way." (Ashton-James, C. E.,& Tracy, J. L. (2012)

Arrogance indicates exaggerated pride. If one is arrogant, he is very likely to compare someone else's achievement against his own, constantly extending his own supremacy. Pride originates out of accountability for certain affirmative and socially valued activity, but arrogance originates from pride not in one's positive activity but in one's "universal self." Certainly, arrogance is regularly referred to as "hubristic" pride. Pride is only positive up to certain level, beyond which it becomes cancerous. Unhealthy exaggerated pride is also known as egotism. For the arrogant person his supposedly great actions are not brought up by effort, but are spontaneous ramification of his enormity. Arrogance is absence of empathy, and hostility toward others.

Unhealthy pride is exceedingly favorable appraisal of one self, basically for a modest achievement the person is giving himself too much acknowledgement related to achievements which are modest at best. This over-estimation of achievements relates to associating successes belonging to others involved in mutual undertaking which victoriously ended.

For a person with unhealthy pride, the matter is not about doing to the best of their abilities, but about doing staff better than anyone else. About their exaggerated achievements they often brag around.

Here's how to make sure that the deadly sin of pride isn't deadly, and authentically helps you be the best possible you:

• Ask, "Who do I want to be?": Not "What do I want?" Or "What will impress other people?" What qualities would you want others to praise at your eulogy?

• Regularly remind yourself: Post-it notes, inspirational pictures, whatever will keep you on track to becoming the best you.

• Focus on effort, not ability: You weren't born with magic powers. But you can get magic results from hard work. And that's something to be proud of (E. Barker, 2017).

Pride in "one's successes might promote positive behaviors in the achievement domain...and contribute to development of a genuine and deep-rooted sense of self-esteem." (Tracy, J. L. & Robins, R. W. (2007)).

NARCISSISM

According mythology Narcissus was a good-looking Greek young man who rejected the advances of the nymph Echo. His punishment was to fall in love with his own reflection in a pool of water. Unable to consummate his love, Narcissus pined away and transformed into the flower named Narcissus.

Psychology and psychiatry, identifies extreme narcissism as a severe personality dysfunction or disorder. Narcissistic personality disorder, otherwise is known as NPD.

Narcissistic Personality Disorder is a psychological disorder characterized by a persistent pattern of grandiosity, fantasies of unlimited power or importance, and the need for admiration or special treatment. Core cognitive, affective, interpersonal, and behavioral features include impulsivity, volatility, attention-seeking, low self-esteem, and unstable interpersonal relationships that result in a pervasive pattern of interpersonal difficulties, occupational problems, and significant psychosocial distress (E. L. Kacel, N. Ennis, and D. B. Pereira, 2018).

The Austrian neurologist Sigmund Freud concluded that narcissism is an essential part of all of us from birth and he was the first to implement the term in reference to psychology.

Psychoanalyst Andrew Morrison claims that, for healthy adult person, a reasonable amount of healthy narcissism allows the individual's perception of his needs to balance with others.

Evolutionary psychology relates Narcissism to psychological mechanisms of mating, or choosing a partner for the purposes of procreation.

Lack of self-insight is a hallmark of narcissism, it suggests that narcissists do not have insight into the negative aspects of their personality or their reputation (e.g., arrogant, disagreeable, entitled). Indeed, narcissists see themselves very positively (e.g., Clifton, Turkheimer, & Oltmanns, 2004) and this motivates them to keep up their overly positive self-perceptions (Morf & Rhodewalt, 2001) which has led researchers to determinate that narcissists "...have less insight into their own condition" (Emmons, 1984, p. 297) and "...probably misunderstand how they are perceived" (Morf & Rhodewalt, 2001, p.183).

One special aspect of narcissists is their ability to make a very positive first impression. At first sight, narcissists reputation is being charming, likeable, extraverted, open to experience, and physically attractive (Back et al., 2010; Friedman, Oltmanns, Gleason, & Turkheimer, 2006; Friedman, Oltmanns, & Turkheimer, 2007; Holtzman & Strube, 2010; Oltmanns, Friedman, Fiedler, & Turkheimer, 2004; Vazire, Naumann, Rentfrow, & Gosling, 2008).

Researchers have noted similarities and differences between high self-esteem and narcissism, two personality constructs involving high level of pride but are associated with divergent cognitive and behavioral repertoires (e.g., Bushman & Baumeister, 1998; Paulhus, Robins, Trzesniewski, & Tracy, 2004; Twenge & Campbell, 2003).

As children, they couldn't get the warmth, care, validation, or support from their caretakers, also they weren't good or worthy enough. To defend against, and hide from, the impoverished self-image, these people fabricated an attitude, mind-set, or demeanour to feel they were actually more worthy than others, perhaps entitled to special treatment. Intimately related to these exaggerated compensatory mechanisms is a literally anti-social tendency to deceive, devalue, debase, and even show disdain for others. These behaviors are mostly unconscious strategies to feel better about themselves, often at others' expense (L. F. Seltzer, 2015).

Narcissists usually present themselves as arrogant, flamboyant, manipulative, pretentious, and often deficient in empathy. Narcissists undertake things above their ability, because they need the commendation arising from doing something others might not do. Thus, all to often people with hubristic pride fail at their undertakings than do those with healthy authentic pride.

Narcissists, sadly often are in leadership positions. Confident, they are better than anyone else, their self-centred moral matrix is self-righteous and accompanied with the belief of superiority.

The abbreviated criteria for Narcissistic Personality Disorder are as follows:

A. Grandiose sense of self-importance or uniqueness.

B. Preoccupation with fantasies of unlimited success, power, brilliance, beauty, or ideal love.

C. Exhibitionist.

D. Cool indifference or marked feelings of rage, inferiority, shame, humiliation, or emptiness in response to criticism, indifference of others, or defeat.

E. At least two of the following generate characteristic disturbances in interpersonal relationships:

1. Entitlement: the expectation of special favors without assuming reciprocal responsibilities;

2. Interpersonal exploitation;

3. Relationships that characteristically alternate between the two extremes of over idealization and devaluation;

4. Lack of empathy (Raskin & Hall, p. 159).

The American Psychiatric Association estimates that less than 1% of the population suffers from Narcissistic Personality Disorder, and from this group, about 50-75% are man (Dobbert, 2007). First and foremost, people high in narcissism have a grandiose sense of self-importance (Brown, Budzek & Tamborski, 2009). They believe they are better than everybody else, and this self-concept, however unrealistic it probably is, guides them in their daily lives (Morf & Rhodewalt, 2001). As Vazire and Funder (2006) suggest, "much of narcissist's, cognitive, affective and behavioral responses are in the service of defending and affirming an unrealistic self-concept.

They are constantly looking for the world to show this notion of grandiosity (Baker, 1979). Narcissistic people depend heavily upon positive feedback from others (Rhodewalt &Morf, 1998) and are not able to tolerate things which threaten the grandiose self, such as negative, critical feedback or failure (Baker, 1979).

Furthermore, narcissistic people tend to attribute success internally and failure externally (Morf & Rhodewalt, 1998, 2001).

Those with narcissistic tendencies are impulsive and can lack self-control (Vazire & Funder, 2006). Narcissistic people may lack the ability to delay pleasurable outcomes in the short-term in favor of gratification in the long run (Robins & Beer, 2001). This impulsivity may actually be biologically linked with low levels of serotonin (Morf & Rhodewalt, 2001). Narcissism and high self-esteem are very highly correlated (r=approximatively 0.40-0.60) (Brown & Bosson, 2001). Both concepts correlate with extroverted personalities, a (sometimes unrealistic) belief that one has "better than average intelligence" (Campbell, 2002). Brown (2009) found a positive correlation between grandiosity, which is a key aspect of narcissism and subjective well-being and mental health, leading him to conclude that some amount of grandiosity, and therefore narcissism is healthy.

Narcissistic people often have high profile leadership jobs, and tend to thrive in them because of their relentless wish for glory, power, and to show how competent they believe they are (Wallace & Baumeister, 2002). They also do better in the public eye than do non-narcissistic people (Young & Pinsky, 2006).

Historically, American presidents have been known to display narcissistic characteristics. For instance, President Franklin Roosevelt was among the most narcissistic of America's presidents, as perceived by the public (Deluga, 1997).

From a practical standpoint, society needs leaders. The American society desires a government full of people who the population admires and wants to follow. Those with narcissistic personalities have tendency for these roles to some extent. Thus, narcissism is at least somewhat beneficial because of inclination to leadership and emergence of leaders (Nevicka, 2011). Conclusion is that narcissism in small amounts is beneficial.

EGOISM

In this chapter, I defend certain unpopular, position: egoism, the notion that we are all always basically motivated by self-interest. Often people are mistaken about what really is in their self-interest. Certainly, people generally rationalize the choice of an existing benefit that turns out not in their self-interest. Nonetheless, sometimes because of the uniting of oneself and another, one can notice that another's interests and his own are blending into bigger interest. Egoism is an interesting psychological phenomenon, which implies with crucial certainty an obscured moral discourse that authentic altruism is an unreasonable ideal.

According to philosophy, egoism is the assumption that one's self is the inspiration and the goal of his own actions. Egoism or self-centredness has two variations: descriptive or normative. The descriptive variation is positive in nature, it conceives egoism as a factual characterization of human affairs. This means a person's encouragement relates to their personal interests and desires. The normative variation proposes that people aspire, regardless of what motivates their behavior now.

Altruism is the complete opposite of egoism. The term "egoism" is derived from "ego," the Latin translation for "I" in English. Egoism is distinguished from egotism, which means a psychological overvaluation of an individual's importance, or of one's own activity.

Two questions arise:

1.   Can one-act only according to his own interests without some regard for others' interests?

2.   Can one-act for other people's interests in complete disregard for his own sphere of interests?

It is understandable that a person has control over their next actions, and, therefore, understandable that one chooses his own actions. Morally speaking, one doesn't even have to ask if the person should pursue his own interests, or, whether he should reject self-interest and pursue other people's interests instead: to what degree are acts done for others morally appreciated compared to self-regarding acts?

I am rejecting authentic altruism, because as do I, as did Lucifer, as do all, we are always pursuing our own self-interest. Of course, I have a concern about other people as well. One can still be cautious in his involvement when it comes to other people, positioning his concern for others on top of his priority list.

Certainly, an individual aware of his self-interest is not selfish or disrespecting towards others, because self-interest takes into account and balances other people's interests as well.

For me, it is difficult to speak about "self-interest", because as Lucifer, it has a very negative reputation (for some people who are definitely not enlightened) often confused with "selfishness." I am proud of myself to try to rehabilitate "selfishness," because it is a worthwhile endeavor. Furthermore, a special form of self-interest is when an individual is inconsiderate to others.

For you, it is important to remember that selfishness is not always in your best interest because you may offend other people close to you, but sometimes you have to, especially when it coincides with your personal best self-interest aligned with your life plan. Especially since when you make your priority self-interest list, you must take into account all your self-interests and how they are influencing others.

I always do what I want, certainly never escaping my ego is in my best interest, because the word "egoism" is implying I am purgative, but this is often complex. The ego ultimately does what it wants, there is no escaping it. I never do what I do not want to and what is not in my self-interest. It is an illusion for one to do what one does not want because to do so necessities for one to put other people's interests above his own which is naïve philosophical discourse.

Michael Slote, argues, "If there is no such thing as (human) altruism, then the altruistic demands of most social codes and most moral philosophies are deeply undermined," and he blames protectors of egoism for "show[ing] precious few signs of recognizing and regretting the destructively iconoclastic direction of their views and arguments."

Actually, supporting your self-interest can relieve your concerns about its negative influence on your life, especially since when all is going well there are no concerns or misgivings.

In Human, All Too Human, Friedrich Nietzsche writes, "No man has ever done anything wholly for others and with no personal motivation whatever; how, indeed, should a man be able to do something that had no reference to himself, that is to say lacked all inner compulsion (which would have its basis in personal need)? How could the ego act without the ego?"

For example, if I do something for others, I would do it because I want to, this means I have personal motivation to do so, thus fallow my ego because it wants to do something. What this means is that the desire motivating my action is still in my self-interest, only not a selfish one.

In Plato's "Republic," Socrates discusses with his older brother Glaucon in which Glaucon insists that people's good behavior actually only exists for self-interest: People only do the right thing because they fear being punished if they get caught. If human actions were invisible to others, Glaucon says, even the most "just" man would act purely for himself and not care if he harmed anyone in the process.

It's the sort of argument which might have appealed to Thomas Hobbes, the 17th-century English philosopher famous for saying that the natural state of man's life would be "nasty, brutish and short." According to Hobbes, humans must form social contracts and governments to prevent their selfish, violent tendencies from taking over. Biologist Michael Ghiselin memorably writes "scratch an altruist, and watch a hypocrite bleed."

Joel Marks, concern is: What we do is always an action, and action is always motivated, and another name for motivation is 'desire'. This means an individual is always conscious of his actions all along recognizing and supporting his self-interest.

Marks is quite confident that we always do what we want to do, but he also considers that what we want to do is not always what we identify as personal self-interest. I ask you now if an action I undertake is not in my self-interest why would I do it?

Again, it is very simple, because ultimately I want to undertake this action, I have internal wish to do so, out of love, regret, shame, disgrace, sense of duty, obligation, etc. To act upon feelings motivating me coincides with my self-interest, but I always discern what is a must and what is not. This means I can not escape my egoism, because escaping it will need for me to act as I have no interest in doing. This finally diminishes the myth of human altruism.

You must embrace your self-interest which will set you on a new path away of failure and continual decline. This doesn't mean that you need to embrace only pleasurable experiences, just to do what you want to do. If taking care of someone close makes you feel good, do that, but only because you have a wish to do so.

Sometimes sacrifice will be what you want to do, especially when it comes to one's children, in cases like this one sacrifice is with conscious deliberation and ultimately is what you want to do. Is sacrifice conceptually rational to egoism? Yes, but only in a limited sense. One can still sacrifice for one's children, even sacrifice one's life. What one can't do is what one does not want to do.

Joshua May asks: "Does it not seem, for example, that your motivation to promote the well-being of your children, say, isn't instrumental to any other desire to help yourself?" Certainly, caring for children is a representation of mutual interest. In this case, empathy takes center stage, to merge the interests in a greater whole. This is when the interests of others are inseparable from oneself.

According to Olson, "Morally valuable acts of self-sacrifice are exemplifications of habit-patterns themselves deliberately cultivated for self-interest" (The Morality of Self-Interest, p. 35).

Is it really possible then, for the egoist to adopt the obvious, and today popular, solution, namely, that his doctrine expresses a conceptual truth? This means that any action, must always conform to at least one condition: it is according to one's own interests. This, however, is a purely formal condition. Consequently, there is no logical limit to what one might consider his own interests. So it is possible for an individual to identify his own interests with those of other people: he might value other people's interests as much as, or more than, his own. But if psychological egoism as a conceptual truth allows this possibility, where is the egoism? To treat it as a conceptual truth is to destroy it (W. D. Glasgow, 1978). This is not correct, because an individual is never focused on other people's interests, but on the mutual interest, thus egoism prevails.

It is fair to conclude that self-interest is what would make a person to live his best possible life.

To see why we inevitably act in our perceived self-interest, consider the question "Why to act in my self-interest?" as baffling, almost nonsensical. The answer is "Because it is in your self-interest." As in the case of the revenge-seeker, people are mistaken about what really is in their self-interest, but not whether they have a good reason to act in their self-interest (David Copp and Jeffrey Paul, 1997).

The details of self-interest will vary considerably from one person to the next and even for the same person across time; one size does not fit all. Self-interest is not strictly identifiable with pleasure or happiness or advantage (Mark Mercer, 1998).

Self-interest does not mean the same as acting wisely; self-interested motivation is a must because being wise is not. All actions are fundamentally self-interested, but not all actions are wise in the sense of being prudent, practical, and well-intendant.

Nietzsche writes in 1989, "anyone who has really made sacrifices knows that he wanted and got something in return."

Similarly, Ayn Rand says, "If a man who is passionately in love with his wife spends a fortune to cure her of a dangerous illness, it would be absurd to claim that he does it as a 'sacrifice' for her sake, not his own."

Robert Olson says, "by praising a man for acting consistently in his own best interests one encourages him to cultivate habits of rationality and rational self-control with all the social advantages which this entails."

It is a bit difficult, although possible to be wise in perusing self-interest with discipline and lucidity.

Olson's Morality of Self-interest states: "[I]f each of us is prepared to make reasonable sacrifices for the sake of more or less distant personal goods, the result would be a state of society in which private and social interests tend to coincide", thus eradicating the 'need' for anyone to make irrational sacrifices for the benefit of other people."

We will never understand how humans make decisions until we recognize that societies are collections of individuals that primarily follow their self-interest.

Nowadays, very few people follow self-interest prudently and some pursue it only declarative, however, all people pursue it. The presented argument showed that egoism does not entail that we can't care for others.

Ego shock refers to feeling mentally paralyzed in response to large self-esteem threats. Individuals who are in a state of ego shock have trouble thinking; they feel far away from themselves; the reality seems distant or weird; they feel emotionally indifferent. Ego shock experience only lasts for few seconds or minutes.

MORAL PHILOSOPHY OF EGOISM

Moral Philosophy is a branch of philosophy that contemplates the rational study of the meaning and justification of moral claims. It researches the concept of morality and studies how people should live their lives in relation to others.

Moral philosophy has three branches. One branch, meta-ethics, investigates big-picture questions, another branch of moral philosophy is normative ethics, which replies the question of what we should do. Normative ethics offer a matrix for deciding what is right and wrong. Allied ethics is also a branch of Moral philosophy, it addresses practical issues of moral importance that can have terminal consequences.

Since the discussion in the earlier chapters focused on certain moral claims related to big-picture questions, I think Moral philosophy can offer a practical framework, especially when applied to specific dilemmas, all in order to offer ethical life.

Morality has become a perplexing topic during the age of world globalization. It defines the basic principles that control human behavior. Morality is often associated with certain religious doctrine, however, this is not always the case. Every person has their own moral principles.

Morality is correlated with human behavior. Acclaimed author C.S. Lewis classifies this relation as:

(1) to make sure fair play and harmony between people; (2) to

help make us good people to have a good society; and

(3) to keep us in a good relationship with the power that created us.

This definition makes it clear that our beliefs are instrumental to our personal moral behavior.

The first two points are understandable observation, but the third point is where most discord arises. Of course most of the people in the world believe in God, nonetheless the issue of creationism versus evolution, defined as a theory of origins, obviously is very debated topic, not only in the academic circles but among the common public as well.

A report in Psychology Today states: "The most significant predictor of a person's moral behavior may be religious commitment. People who consider themselves very religious were least likely to report deceiving their friends, having extramarital affairs, cheating on their expenses accounts, or even parking illegally."

According to the above, personal believes about the creation of life have a critical influence over our thinking, behavior and moral in general. If we do not believe in God, we will then have to make up moral standards at our own personal convenience. This standards than can result in conflict and chaos. Morality influences our actions and decisions, all along free will controls those preferences.

Regarding the origin of consciousness Paul the Apostle, writes that even the unbelievers adhere to the laws of God as stated in the Ten Commandments: "for when Gentiles, who do not have the law, by nature do the things in the law, these, although not having the law, are a law to themselves, who show the work of the law written in their hearts, their conscience also bearing witness, and between themselves their thoughts accusing or else excusing them" (Romans 2:14-15, NKJV).

According to New World Encyclopaedia, 2019, Meta-ethics determinate the nature of judgments of moral right or wrong, good and bad. It is not concerned with finding out which actions or things are right and wrong, or which states are good and bad, but with understanding the nature and meaning of concepts of right and wrong, good and bad. Normative ethics are concerned with moral norms.

A moral norm is a norm in the sense of being a standard with which moral agents ought to comply. Normative ethics have two central concepts: The right and the morally good. The concept of the right is, roughly, the concept of duty, the concept of which actions we ought to do, and which it would be wrong not to do.

The theory of right action asks a crucial question in Normative ethics, what is right and what is wrong? This theory is giving the answer to the question "What one must do from a moral standpoint"? Utility is a basic moral principle according to which right actions and decisions are those that augment happiness. In Kantianism, the imperative is an essential principle from which right actions are derivative to duties.

Virtue theory focuses on what states of character are morally desirable. This theory does not explore actions, but character and its traits. Basic human traits that bring benefit to other people like good, courageous, strong, and virtuous, relate in a positive light and are praiseworthy.

According to Classical utilitarianism, right action is ought to produce the greatest balance of general happiness. Thus, the theory is promoting hedonism as the right course of action and as a theory of value, with the principle utility a central motive. Nowadays, this theory mainly focuses on the valuable state of interest.

The famous German philosopher Immanuel Kant has been enormously influential with his work based on a moral principle from which all our responsibilities derive. This is a principle of consistency, demanding that we act according to rotational reasons, which take into account the respect for other people.

The most famous theorist in ethical intuitionism is W.D. Ross, who theorizes a number of exclusive moral responsibilities (such as, loyal, to refrain from harming people, to keep your word, etc.), all of which are important in their own right. Ross believes that the right action in particular circumstances is balancing of different moral principles.

Virtue ethics distances itself from theorizing over the right action and focuses on virtuous character. Actually, virtue ethics attempts to describe what attributes are desirable and then tends to characterize right actions in conditions of these attributes called virtues. Certainly, to consider an individual as virtuous he needs to act correctly in any situation, all along perceiving rightly the situation. Different situations, in different conditions, will so cause different behavior.

Moral philosophy defines the moral rules and principles, hence providing clear guidance for definite action in a particular situation.

According to Plato, the soul's main attributes are knowledge of universal truth in the shape of eudaimonia (happiness or well-being) resulting from virtue based on the good that belongs only to God. Aristotle believed eudaimonia is the highest of all goods, which, relishes in the life of God.

It is understandable in the historical context that God is referred to as the pedestal of morality. According to divine command theory, moral values depend on God. Philosophical ethicists such as Philip L. Quinn and Robert M. Adams uphold this theory. However, the divine command theory received a lot of criticism over time and it does not have many supporters.

THE UNCERTAINTY OF MEANING

L ord Michel Eyquem de Montaigne who was one of the most significant philosophers of the french renaissance has a famous statement: "Life in itself is neither good nor evil. It is the place of good and evil, according to what you make it."

A person as a rational being which easily escapes the dangers of the natural hardly predictable world, nonetheless he is never free, even though he presents consciousness. As long as there have been people and as long as they have lived, the uncertainty of their existence is constant. Since the past is no longer here, the future is ambiguous by definition, the only certain thing one holds in his hand is the present moment. The next present moment there might be another certain thing and so on. However, the non-temporal truth is that the present moment is mainly inconsequential in the large scheme of the multi individual environment, as part of a collective, where all the people are influencing each other and interact with the environment as well. Here is the trap, actually, one must always be careful not to get lost in the immense collective.

It is in the knowledge of the uncertainty of our everyday existence that we must draw the force and strength necessary to outsmart the ambiguity. Basically, existentialism is a theory of ambiguity, but some philosophers define existentialism as a theory of absurd and despair. It is making choices about existential questions that bring anguish in an individual's life. Avoiding this anguish will necessitate for an individual to do as he pleases, all the while being attentive and calculated about the possible risks involved with his voluntary actions. His action is as he pleases, but the deliberate intention must take into account the possible failure and balance the performance aspect of the undertaking.

The German philosopher Hegel writes in the closing part of the Phenomenology of Mind that moral consciousness can happen only to the extent that there is antagonism between nature and morality. Consciousness would dissipate if the ethical law became the natural law. The paradoxical "displacement," is that if moral action is the absolute goal, the absolute goal may not have the moral action present. This means that there is being who questions himself in his being, and is a being who is distanced from himself and who is his being.

A person can not say that our earthly prospects have or have not importance, because it depends on him to give it significance. It is up to oneself to make one's life important, and he alone can determinate his success or failure.

Marxism defines the goal and essence of human action by wills, these wills do not materialize as free. They are contemplation of certain conditions of the circumstances of the people under examination.

However, in my opinion, freedom is the point of origin from which all assurances and all values arise. It is the original position of all confirmation of existence. The man who pursues to rationalize his life must put freedom above all else. Freedom requires the realization of specific actions, taken upon concrete assignment. It is the danger of losing your freedom that will make you understand its existence.

Descartes said that the freedom of man is limitless, however, he has limited power. The power of the person when annulled is not limited, because zero is not a number of value.

An individual's freedom will not come to anguish against an obstacle, because it will still pursue its goal even in the face of immediate failure, by giving itself a factual content, and continual aiming for the free development of existence. Freedom gives meaning to life that itself is naturally drawn to find the will to live.

One should know that his freedom is not an abstract concept, and recognize that at the moment he frees his hands from something he had held tight, he will have them up in the air, a condition that guarantees the greatest freedom. When an individual is constantly free, it allows for the will to show the true being of oneself.

THE PHILOSOPHY OF FREEDOM

The Philosophy of Freedom is a book by Rudolf Steiner that basically explains the process of thinking as an activity through which external reality enters inside of us and individualizes our personal relationship with the world. According to Steiner thinking is an intuitive experience of the true nature of our being and acting upon the thinking manifests our core. Our core drive is the search for the meaning of our life in a specific moment.

The thinking extents out above our personal existence and gives account to the broad world existence, increasing the universal desire for knowledge in us. It is understandable that beings without thinking do not posses desire. It is during thinking that internal concept rises up and brings knowledge to the front. But knowledge itself is the other side of the concept because it represents only one perception of reality.

These are the opening lines of Volkelt's book on Immanuel Kant's Theory of Knowledge: What is here put forward as an immediate and self-evident truth is really the result of a thought operation which runs as follows: The naïve person believes things, just as he perceives them, that they exist outside of our consciousness. Our perception modifies our organization. This thinking was also elaborated by Eduard von Hartmann who believes that an individual can have direct knowledge only of his conceived reality.

The father of modern philosophy, Descartes, based the entire human knowledge in one sentence: I think, therefore I am. All other existence is independent of my own. According to him, he is absolutely certain, he exists.

Obviously, observation occurs before thinking, because we first see and then think. However, one can not see himself while he is thinking. A person possessing naïve consciousness regards thinking as something immaterial. He treats the objects of external experience as his realities. For the naïve man it is proof enough of his reality that "Nothing exists that cannot be perceived" is, in fact, the first axiom of the naïve man; and similarly "Everything perceived exists." However, this is a primitive form of believing only in what is physically manifested, because man can perceive it. According to Steiner "The mental picture is an individualized concept." Thinking, in its basic nature, has the real I or ego, but it does not contain the ego-consciousness. But the same concept, or perception, affects different people in a different way. Steiner continues that the person first perceives, then this translates itself directly into willing, without the intervention of either a feeling or a concept. The driving force here involved is simply called instinct. The satisfaction of our lower, primal animal needs (hunger, sexual intercourse, etc.) comes about in this way. An important characteristic of instinctive life is that immediately the perception releases the act of will.

Rudolf Steiner then goes on to say: The mental picture of one's own or another's welfare is, however, rightly regarded as a motive of the will. The principle of producing the greatest quantity of pleasure for oneself through one's action, to achieve personal happiness, is egoism. Attainment of happiness sought either by thinking ruthlessly only of one's own good and striving to attain it even at the cost of the happiness of other people (pure egoism), or by promoting the good of others, either because one anticipates a favorable influence on one's own person indirectly through the happiness of others, or because one fears to endanger one's own interest by injuring others (morality of prudence). The special content of the egotistical principles of morality will depend on the mental pictures which we form of what is our own, or other's happiness. He then concludes: Only when I follow my love for my aim it is I who act. This implies that determination is the principle element of free will. Rudolf Steiner condition for freedom is: Man is free in so far as he is able to obey himself in every moment of his life.

The truth is an individual's life consists of free and unfree actions. Which of us can confidently say that he is really free in his life? Yet in each of us, there is a deeper being where the free man finds his expression.

Desiring gives pleasure by itself. There is enjoyment found in the hope of a remote but hearty desired goal. This joy also contains all the labor that gives us results only in the future. It is a pleasure that is separate from the attainment of the aim. After reaching the goal, the pleasure of fulfillment adds to the pleasure of desiring. Obviously, the fulfillment of a desire brings pleasure with itself and its nonfulfillment brings pain.

The man tosses back upon himself. It is he who gives his action intention. If he looks in the external for the grounds that give direction to his will, he will see in vain. If he is to go beyond merely satisfying his natural instincts, then he must seek these grounds in his own moral principles, unless he finds it more convenient to let himself be determined by the moral principles of others, actually, he must stop his action altogether, or else he must act for reasons that others choose for him out of their interest. In this manner, a Man is the last determinant of his action. He is forever free, only his freedom is found in his actions. When a man is free from false needs and dependence on the world he can make it to the top.

NAIVE REALISM

The Problem of Perception posses the greatest chasm in whole philosophy. How can it be for the perceptual experience to transfer into an openness to the thought independent world? Is it that some personal experiences are themselves in their essence not an authentic representation of the relations to ordinary objects? Or in fact, they are not representing the relations to ordinary objects.

Naive realism is a theory belonging to the philosophy of mind, established as a common-sense theory of perception. It describes people's inclination to trust they see the social world "as it is" or representation of objective reality, instead of a subjective creation and interpretation of reality. This blind trust that individual's perceptions are realistic, not prejudiced interpretations of the social world has two real implications. First of these implications is that highly rational people will have very much alike perception of reality as myself. Second, other people who have different perceptions of reality from myself are ignorant (i.e., not privy to the same information as me), irrational, and partial.

Perception is a subjective construction of the social world instead of direct representation of objective reality. Consequently, people's notions and perceptions correlate both the objective world and the cognitive processes that transform those objective characteristics into psychologically advanced characteristics. Naive realists want to keep up awareness of our ordinary conception of perceptual experience.

Lee Ross had explained a few important implications of naïve realism. First one is that since people believe their perceptions are real, it follows that other reasonable people who have the same experience will share the same perceptions. This proposition is the reason why people project their own assumptions, convictions, beliefs, feelings, and assessment on to other people.

Our ordinary conception of perceptual experience is a form of "openness to the world" McDowell (1994: 111). P.F. Strawson disagreed, reflection on ordinary perceptual experience holds a characterization in terms of Mind-Independence: "mature sensible experience (in general) presents itself as, in the Kantian phrase, an immediate consciousness of the existence of things outside us" (1979: 97).

This argument strengthens if we present what French and Walters termed as the Exclusion Assumption (cf., Snowdon (1992: 74)):

If the illusion of an ordinary object presents as F the person is aware of an F thing which is not identical to the ordinary object, in this case, the person is not likewise aware of the ordinary object. The conclusion is: it is an illusory experience when one is aware of an F thing non-identical to the ordinary observed object.

Veridical experiences involved in cases of perception, where a person sees or in another way perceives an object for what it actually is for naïve realists-are experiences of awareness to the perceived objects.

Naive realists think of the experience as not representational in a sense that what is basic to experience is something which cannot be explained as representing the world.

We can suppose that if the certain experience is of subject-matter from a specific viewpoint (Martin, (1998)), or standpoint (Campbell, (2009)), then variation in what goes into one having the particular viewpoint or standpoint should make for variation in the phenomenal character. Many naïve realists believe that there is variation in the way one relates to a subject-matter which changes the phenomenal character (Soteriou, (2013), Campbell, (2014)).

From Naive realism, it follows that perception is what establishes your reality. Hence, if you change your perception you will change your reality. If you change your reality, you will change your life. If you change your life, you will change your destiny. And some destinies are here to change the world we live in.

DIGNITY

Human dignity has a growing role and holds a prominent place in contemporary philosophy, ethics, bioethics, and human rights instruments. I will present the major archetypes of dignity that everyone has inherent worth and concomitant rights and will point out that the idea of dignity has a valuable role as a moral standard. Human dignity or human worthiness has been an idea worth studying by many cultures and civilizations from ancient times until today. Five major archetypes of dignity have developed the value that modern cultures adhere to every person: moral dignity (antiquity), spiritual dignity (Middle Ages and Renaissance), rational dignity (seventeenth and eighteenth centuries), social dignity (nineteenth century), and human dignity stricto sensu (twentieth and twenty-first centuries). These archetypes are methodological tools with specific features that help scientists to understand dignity.

Human beings are unique in their rationality and free will and posses moral framework of good and evil. Plato thought that the human soul (psyché) has a divine origin (Timaeus, 90a-b), and its proper goal is to reach justice and goodness through cognitive rationality and contemplation (The Republic, 353d3-13). Aristotle also stated the specific worth of human beings, underlining rationality as of a divine origin (On the Soul, 408b15).

Roman philosophers, Cicero and Seneca, developed a notion,

which explained "otherness" and the idea that all man are born equal. Cicero refers to the term dignity as excellence and dignity (excellentia et dignitas). Seneca proposes an equal dignity of all people, his sentence homo homini sacra res ("man is a sacred thing for man") ("Letter XCV," in the Moral Letters to Lucilius) recognizes that everyone in itself is the basis of humankind.

The phrase of dignitas hominis defends and celebrates the excellence and greatness (excellentia ac praestantia) of humans. The positive perspective of the dignitas hominis is a reaction against the pessimistic thoughts on human existence. Great thinkers like Giovanni Pico della Mirandola, Francesco Petrarca, Bartolomeo Fazio, Giannozzo Manetti, Marsilio Ficino, Giordano Bruno, Erasmus of Rotterdam, and Juan Luis Vives, had different approaches, nonetheless their works developed the concept of dignitas hominis, representing human beings as a "magnum miraculum" (a great miracle), which encompasses all the laws and principles of the expanding universe and its nature (microcosmos). For many of the renaissance philosophers including Pico della Mirandola the humans have no purposeful substance or nature but are given freedom and intelligence to make their destiny and their selves, in a sense you are what you make from yourself.

In the seventeenth century, philosophers René Descartes and Blaise Pascal asserted the dignity of humans who possess a rational nature. For Pascal, the dignity of humans ultimately is found in their lucidity of the greatness of their nature: "the greatness of a man is great in that he knows himself is miserable" (Thoughts, 105).

In the seventeenth century, Grotius referred to the "excellence and dignity of man" whose reason enables him to progress and understand the greatest truths of mundane and social life (De jure belli ac pacis, "Preliminary Address," § IX). In the same course of thinking, Pufendorf attributes the "dignity and excellence of man (.. .), which requires that he conforms his actions to a [legal] norm." Humans are "endued with the light of understanding, with the faculties of judging and of choosing things, and with an admirable capacity for arts and knowledge" (De jure naturae et gentium, 95).

In the eighteenth century, German philosopher Immanuel Kant writes that "idea of the dignity of a rational being who obeys no law except that which it at the same time gives" (Groundwork for the Metaphysics of Morals, 424). Kant notes: "Act only according to that maxim whereby you can, at the same time, will that it should become a universal law" (Groundwork, 421). He then concludes: "Act in such a way that you treat humanity, whether in your own person or in the person of any other, never merely as a means and always at the same time as an end" (Groundwork, 429).

In the nineteenth century the aim of dignity from individualistic becomes universal, it is dignity from which human rights derive. The dignity of human beings "stricto sensu" is a universal ethical and legal principle which proposes that all humans are worthy and have rights only because they are human.

After the Second World War, the Universal Declaration of Human Rights (UDHR) (1948), served as fundamental international human rights system, based on the "recognition of the inherent dignity and of the equal and inalienable rights of all members of the human family" (Preamble). According to the Declaration "all human beings are born free and equal in dignity and rights" (Article 1).

With the Declaration dignity of human beings is now formally integrated into national and international legal systems. According to the UDHR all humans are "free and equal in dignity and rights", and "these rights derive from the inherent dignity of the human person" (1966 International Covenants on Civil and Political Rights, and on Economic, Social and Cultural Rights, Preambles).

SELF-ESTEEM

People try to make sense of the souranding world, always striving to feel complete. The main notion of self-esteem is to feel, imagine and present to the world what one has thought and believed about himself. Self-esteem relates to internal self-assessment which can go either way, positive or negative, this depends on personal believes construct on perception and evaluation. Self-esteem also refers to a human being's individual estimation of his personal worth.

The preservation and improvement of self-esteem have always been recognized as a fundamental human impulse. Philosophers, authors, educators, and psychologists all have accentuated the fundamental role of self-image in encouragement, influence, and social interactions.

The term self-esteem means "reverence for self." The "self" pertains to the values, beliefs, and attitudes we hold about ourselves. Having a strong will and self-confidence, decision-making power, originality, creativity, sanity and mental health is directly related to self-esteem and sense of self-worth. It also refers to an individual's sense of his or her value or worth, or the extent to which a person values, approves of, appreciates, prizes, or likes him or herself.

During childhood, if an individual was respected, thoughts

valued and abilities recognized than self-esteem strengthens. When feelings trampled upon, thoughts belittled and ability criticized than the individual's self-esteem remains at a low point of development and weak. During the course of time, an individual faces many life situations. Depending upon the success or failure and one's reaction to every significant situation in life, self-esteem grows stronger or gets considerably weakened. Self-esteem is the evaluation that one makes about oneself, based on one's self-worth (L. Noronha, M. Monteiro, and N. Pinto, 2018).

According to Nicholas Elmer self-esteem is about psychological health, about motivations, about personal identity. Perhaps the most striking and distinctive feature of contemporary usage, however, is the idea that self-esteem is a kind of resource or asset. And, like other assets, it is now discussed within the realm of human rights. People want self-esteem, just as they want prosperity, good physical health, or freedom of thought. But they also regard it as something they should have by right. And, if they lack self-esteem, this is because they are denied or deprived of it through the actions or inactions of others.

William James in his Principles of Psychology, published in 1890: self-esteem is success divided by pretensions. This notion has some interesting implications. Self-esteem can be increased by achieving greater successes and maintained by avoiding failures, but it can also be increased by adopting less ambitious goals: 'to give up pretensions is as blessed a relief as to get them gratified' (James, 1890, p. 311). James explains that self-esteem cannot be predicted from the objective level of success a human being accomplishes. What is important is that personal successes are relevant to personal aspirations.

Different studies have concluded that self-esteem relates to our overall well-being. Self-esteem expert Morris Rosenberg concludes that self-esteem is simply one's attitude toward oneself (1965). Rosenberg described human's self-esteem as a "favorable or unfavorable attitude toward the self".

Different factors influence self-esteem among which: genetics, personality, life circumstances, age, overall health, thinking, social circumstances, the reactions of others and comparing oneself to other people.

Self-esteem is a similar concept to self-worth but with a small (although important) difference: self-esteem is what we think, feel, and believe about ourselves, while self-worth is the more global recognition that we are valuable human beings worthy of love (Hibbert, 2013).

Self-esteem refers to the degree to which we accept and approve of ourselves. It is actually the overall sense of respect we have for ourselves. Self-esteem always includes evaluation and we can have a positive or negative opinion of ourselves.

When we compare ourselves to others and find that we are better at something than others and/or that people respond favorably to what we do, our self-esteem in that area grows. On the other hand, when we compare ourselves to others and find we're not as successful in a given area and/or people respond negatively to what we do, our self-esteem decreases (C. Vinney, 2018).

Self-esteem is not self-confidence; self-confidence is about your trust in yourself and your ability to deal with challenges, solve problems, and engage successfully with the world (Burton, 2015). In this manner, self-confidence bases are external measures of success and worth, rather than the internal values that contribute to self-esteem.

We know that people with high self-esteem:

- Appreciate themselves and other people.

- Enjoy growing as a person and finding fulfillment and meaning in their lives.

- Are able to dig deep within themselves and be creative.

- Make their own decisions and conform to what others tell them and act only when they agree.

- See the word in realistic terms, accepting other people the way they are, all along pushing them toward greater confidence and a more positive direction.

•	Can easily concentrate on solving problems in their lives.

•	Have loving and respectful relationships.

•	Know what their values are and live their lives accordingly.

•	Speak up and tell others their opinions, calmly and kindly, and share their wants and needs with others.

•	Endeavor to make a constructive difference in other people's lives (Smith & Harte, n.d.).

An individual with high self-esteem:

•	Act assertively without experiencing any guilt, and feels at ease communicating with others.

•	Avoids dwelling on the past and focuses on the present moment.

•	Believes one is equal to everyone else, no better and no worse.

•	Rejects the attempts of others to manipulate him.

•	Recognizes and accepts a range of feelings, both positive and negative, and shares those within his healthy relationships.

•	Enjoys a healthy balance of work, play, and relaxation.

•	Accepts challenges and takes risks to grow, and learn from his mistakes when he fails.

•	Handles criticism without taking it personally, with the knowledge that he is learning and growing and that his worth is not dependent on the opinions of others.

•	Values himself and communicates well with others, without fear of expressing his likes, dislikes, and feelings.

•	Values others and accepts them as they are without trying to change them (Self Esteem Awareness, n.d.).

Recent research done on university students from Brazil concluded that there is a correlation between self-esteem and optimism (Bastianello, Pacico & Hutz & 2014).

Self-esteem researcher and expert Dr. John M. Grohol outlined six practical tips on how to increase your sense of self-esteem, which include:

1.   Take a self-esteem inventory to give yourself a baseline.

It is as simple as writing down 10 of your strengths and 10 of your weaknesses. This will help you to begin developing an honest and realistic concept of yourself.

2.   Set realistic expectations.

It's important to set small, reachable goals that are within your ability. For instance, setting an extremely high expectation or an expectation that someone else will change their behavior, is almost guaranteed to make you feel like a failure, through no fault of your own.

3.   Stop being a perfectionist and acknowledge both your accomplishments and mistakes.

Nobody is perfect, and trying so will only lead to disappointment. Acknowledging your accomplishments and recognizing your mistakes, is the way to keep a positive outlook while learning and growing from your mistakes.

4.   Explore yourself.

Knowing yourself and being at peace with who you are cannot be overstated. This can take some trial and error, and you will constantly learn new things about yourself, but it is a journey that is undertaken with purpose and zeal.

5.   Be willing to adjust your self-image.

We all change as we age and grow, and we must keep up with our ever-changing selves if we want to set and achieve meaningful goals.

6.   Stop comparing yourself to others.

Comparing ourselves to others is a trap that is extremely easy to fall into, especially today with social media and the ability to project a polished, perfected appearance. The only person you should compare yourself to is you (Grohol, 2011).

This is a list which comes from the Entrepreneur website, it has specific and practical advice on what you can do to develop and maintain self-esteem:

• Use distancing pronouns. When you are experiencing stress or negative self-talk, try putting it in more distant terms (e.g., instead of saying "I am feeling ashamed," try saying "Courtney is feeling ashamed."). This can help you to see the situation as a challenge and not a threat.

• Remind yourself of your achievements. The best way to overcome imposter syndrome—the belief that, despite all of your accomplishments, you are a failure and a fraud—is to list all of your personal successes. You might be able to explain a couple of them away as a chance, but they can't all be due to luck!

• Move more! This is as simple as a short walk or as intense as a several-mile run, as quick as striking a "power pose" or as long as a two-hour yoga session; it doesn't matter exactly what you do, just that you get more in touch with your body and improve both your health and your confidence.

• Use the "five-second" rule. No, not the one about food dropped on the ground! This five-second rule is about following up good thoughts and inspiring ideas with action. Do something to make that great idea happen within five seconds.

• Practice visualizing your success. Close your eyes and take a few minutes to imagine the scenario where you have reached your goals, using all five senses and paying attention to the details.

• Be prepared—for whatever situation you are about to meet. If you are going into a job interview, make sure you have practiced, know about the company, and have some good questions ready to ask. If you are going on a date, take some time to boost your confidence, dress well, and have a plan A and a plan B (and maybe even a plan C!) to make sure it goes well.

•	Limit your usage of social media. Spend less time looking at a screen and more time experiencing the world around you.

•	Meditate. Establish a regular meditation practice to inspect your thoughts, observe them, and separate yourself from them. Cultivating a sense of inner peace will go a long way towards developing healthy self-esteem.

•	Keep your goals a secret. You don't need to keep all of your hopes and dreams to yourself, but make sure you save some of your goal striving and success for just you—it can make you more likely to meet them and more satisfied when you do.

•	Practice affirmations. Make time to regularly say positive things about yourself in situations in which you often feel uncertain.

•	Build your confidence through failure. Use failure as an opportunity to learn and grow, and seek failure by trying new things and taking calculated risks (Laurinavicius, 2017).

Various studies concluded that social media usage negatively impacts self-esteem (Friedlander, 2016).

Facebook, Instagram, and Twitter are not representing life, only the perfect picture, without a place for depression, sadness, failure, and disappointment that are building blocks of human life.

SELF-RESPECT

Self-Respect is a form of self-love wherein a person values his or her own unique approach to living Life.

It is having an understanding and appreciation of the underlying character traits of one's True Self—and most importantly—making life choices and decisions from that authentic aspect of a person's personality. This is very different from relying on one's ego or False Self persona that serves as a cover to show the world only "the good stuff" of a person's personality (H. Vierra, 2018).

Gaining self-respect is about learning your worth, knowing your value, and advocating for yourself, as needed. Self-respect is important for making mature decisions that impact your life and the lives of others connected to you. At the end of the day, self-respect starts with you so you can have better interpersonal relationships (D. Matthews, 2018).

So what is self-respect? It's the belief that you are worthy of love, attention, and respect, and you are no less than anyone else.

Given this belief, you set boundaries with others, essentially drawing a line about how you will and will not be treated (J. D. Matthews, 2018).

Self-respect is a state of recognition that a person is just as important and worthy as any other human or sentient being on the planet. One person is no more or less important but is significant nonetheless (L. Larsen, 2018).

Self-respect is the ability of an individual to know his self-worth and also an expectation of respectful treatment by others. When you have self-respect it helps for others to see and treat you with dignity all along acknowledging your worth.

Often the bases of self-respect are being aware of your intimate values and being able to stand by your character. People with self-respect are willing to defend their actions.

Self-respect is very important for positive mind-set it is the fundamental belief system and correlated actions that confirm we are worthy of appreciation by other people. It is the main reason for obtaining healthy relationships because only people who respect their selves are able to give and receive love.

Self-respect plays a major role in attaining and maintaining healthy romantic relationships. In order for love to exist, respect is necessary. Especially since one must have healthy boundaries and appreciation for himself to create space in a romantic relationship.

Other people treat us as we allow them to, this is why we must build and keep up healthy self-respect. Often unconsciously, we teach others how to treat us, based on our thoughts and feelings about ourselves, it is critical that if we want success in our lives it begins with respecting ourselves. Also, we need consciousness about who we let in our inner circle because those are the people who influence our belief-system, which ultimately influences our decisions and behavior. It is important for one never to allow himself the position, second-best to anyone because if you don't stand for yourself you will fall for anything. Most often you are the result of the choices you make, this is why empowerment, related to love and respect of yourself including your faults and strengths, matter. Life will reward you when you live freely as being yourself.

SELF-IMAGE

Self-image relates to how we see and understand ourselves on a more universal level (internally and externally). Random House Dictionary characterizes self-image as "the idea, conception, or mental image one has of oneself." The Mountain State Centre for Independent Living describes: "Self-image is how you perceive yourself. It is a number of self-impressions that have built up over time... Those self-images are very positive, giving a person confidence in their thoughts and actions, or negative, making a person doubtful of their capabilities and ideas." What you perceive with your eyes when you look at yourself in the mirror and how you conceive yourself in your head is actually your self-image.

Self-image is a representation of our personal understanding of reality, construct during our life, it is a variable that changes as we do. Thus we have influence and control over our self-image.

Self-image correlates to self-concept, where self-concept is a more general than self-image; it involves how you see yourself, how you think about yourself, and how you feel about yourself. In a sense, self-image is one of the components that make up self-concept (McLeod, 2008).

Self-image is like self-concept in that it is all about how you see yourself (McLeod, 2008). Instead of being real, self-image, bases on false believes about ourselves. Our personal self-image is close to reality, but it is always subjective and out of line with objective reality or with the way other people perceive us.

Self-compassion centers on how we relate to ourselves and not how we judge or perceive ourselves (Neff, n.d.).

All people look at the world differently. Two people can have completely the same experience but have very different interpretations of the events. Fundamental beliefs are deeply held beliefs that greatly influence how we interpret events.

According to expert Roy Baumeister: "The term 'identity' refers to the definitions that are created for and superimposed on the self" (1997, p. 681).

Identity is the complete impression of our belief of who we are, nevertheless, self-image is only one piece of the puzzle.

Prospective types and dimensions of self-image, that Suzaan Oltmann defined:

The three elements of a person's self-image are:

1.	The way a person perceives or thinks of him/herself.

2.	The way a person interprets others' perceptions (or what he thinks others think) of him/herself.

3.	The way a person would like to be (his ideal self).

The six dimensions of a person's self-image are:

4.	Physical dimension: how a person evaluates his or her appearance;

5.	Psychological dimension: how a person evaluates his or her personality;

6.	Intellectual dimension: how a person evaluates his or her intelligence;

7.	Skills dimension: how a person evaluates his or her social and technical skills;

8.	Moral dimension: how a person evaluates his or her values and principles;

9.   Sexual dimension: how a person feels he or she fits into society's masculine/feminine norms (Oltmann, 2014)

A positive self-image means perceiving yourself as a good-looking and desirable person, also as a resourceful and intelligent person. It also means looking at yourself as a happy and healthy person. The closer you are to your ideal version the more positive self-image you have.

Some positive quotes on self-image are as follows:

"Self-esteem is like a battery. When the battery is charged, the person is positive; when the battery is low, the individual is negative."

Lilly Harry

"A strong, positive self-image is the best possible preparation for success."

Joyce Brothers

"The 'self-image' is the key to human personality and human behavior. Change the self-image and you change the personality and the behavior."

Maxwell Maltz

"It's like everyone tells a story about themselves inside their own head. Always. All the time. That story makes you what you are. We build ourselves out of that story."

Patrick Rothfuss

"Human beings are not born once and for all on the day their mothers give birth to them, but ... life obliges them over and over again to give birth to themselves."

Gabriel García Márquez

"Seeing, feeling, thinking, believing—these are the stages of how we change our style on the outside and our self-image on the inside."

Stacey London

"Too many people overvalue what they are not and undervalue what they are."

Malcolm S. Forbes

"Remember always that you not only have the right to be an individual, you have an obligation to be one."

Eleanor Roosevelt

"Relentless, repetitive self-talk is what changes our self-image."

Denis Waitley

"Believe what is in the line of your needs, for only by such belief is the need fulfilled...Have faith that you can successfully make it, and your feet are nerved to its accomplishment".

William James

"I have done this, says my memory. I cannot have done that, says my pride, remaining inexorable. Finally—memory yields."

Friedrich Nietzsche

"The art of being wise is the art of knowing what to overlook."

William James

"There is nothing worse than self-deception —when the deceiver is at home and always with you."

Plato

SELF-CONCEPT

Self-concept, in general, refers to how a person thinks about, evaluates or perceives themselves. Actually, being aware of oneself means to have a self-concept.

Purkey (1988) describes self-concept as: "the totality of a complex, organized, and dynamic system of learned beliefs, attitudes and opinions that each person holds being true about his or her personal existence".

According to Carl Rogers, self-concept is an overarching construct and self-esteem is one of the components of it (McLeod, 2008).

Self-concept is the individual's belief about himself or herself, including the person's attributes and who and what the self is (Baumeister, 1999). Self-concept is generally thought of as our individual perceptions of our behavior, abilities, and unique characteristics. It is essentially a mental picture of who you are as a person (K. Cherry, 2018). Generally, self-concept replies the question "Who am I?" In this manner, our own awareness of who we are is the concept of our self.

Self-concept constructs from our self-awareness and it develops as we expand our ideas related to who we are.

Lewis (1990) suggests that the development of a concept of self has two aspects:

1.	The Existential Self: This is 'the most basic part of the self-scheme or self-concept; the sense of being separate and distinct from others and the awareness of constancy of the self' (Bee, 1992).

2.	The Categorical Self: In early childhood, an individual realizes that he is also an object in the world.

Carl Rogers (1959) concludes that the self-concept has three separate components:

1	The view you have of yourself (self-image)

2	How much worth you place on yourself (self-esteem or self-worth)

3	What you wish you were really like (ideal-self)

According to the book "Essential Social Psychology" by Richard Crisp and Rhiannon Turner:

1	The individual self consists of attributes and personality traits that separate us from other people. Examples are introversion or extroversion.

2	The relational self represents our relationships with significant others. For example siblings, friends, and spouses.

3	The collective self reflects our role in social groups. For example Canadian, Democrat, African-American, or gay.

Psychologist Dr.Bruce A. Bracken in 1992 defined six specific domains related to self-concept:

Social: the ability to interact with others;

Competence: the ability to meet basic needs;

Affect: the awareness of emotional states;

Physical: feelings about looks, health, physical condition, and overall appearance;

Academic: success or failure in school;

Family: how well one functions within the family unit.

Psychologist Carl Rogers defined three separate parts of self-concept:

1.   Self-image, or how an individual sees himself. Each individual's self-image consists of attributes like physical characteristics, personality traits, and social roles. Self-image is not usually realistic.

2.   Self-esteem, or how much an individual value himself. Many factors can influence self-esteem, including how we compare ourselves to other people and how they react to us.

3.   Ideal self, or how an individual wishes he could be. Often, the way we see ourselves and how we would like to do not match up.

Carl Rogers believed that all people tend to distort reality to some degree, congruence happens when self-concept is fairly aligned with reality. Incongruence occurs when reality doesn't match our self-concept.

According to self-perception theory, acquiring self-knowledge happens the same way as we acquire knowledge about other people: we observe our own behaviors and conclude who we are from our observation.

SELF-IMPORTANCE

V alue is found in self-identity, Aristotle wrote, "Knowing yourself is the beginning of all wisdom." What is this self (or identity) that is so valuable? Self and identity researchers have believed for a long time that the self is both a product of situations and a tool for behavior in situations. Making sense of oneself or who one is, is the path one should take in the world as a fundamental self-project. Self and identity theories conclude that people do care about themselves, want to know who they are, and can use this self-knowledge to make sense of reality. Self and identity influence what people have motivation to do, the way of thinking and to make sense of themselves and others, the actions they undertake, and their feelings, also the ability to control or regulate themselves (Baumeister, 1998; Brewer, 1991; Brown, 1998; Carver & Scheier, 1990; Higgins, 1987, 1989; Oyserman, 2007).

Just as there are different self-concepts, identity theorists vary in how to conceptualize how many identities a person is likely to have. Much as James (1890/1927) described multiple selves, predicting that people have as many selves as they have interaction partners, identity and social identity theorists confer multiple identities based in multiple situations. Identity theorists (Stryker, 1980; Stryker & Burke, 2000) concentrate on how cross-situational stability of identity content appears. From this aspect, identities are distinct parts of the self-concept, the internalized meanings, and expectations associated with the positions one holds in social networks and the roles one plays. In comparison, social identity theorists (Abrams, 1999; Onorato & Turner, 2002; Tajfel, 1981; Tajfel & Turner, 2004) centre on cross-situational malleability. In its strongest formulation, social identity theories conclude that in each interpersonal interaction, people take upon a different identity (see Owens et al., 2010).

In thinking about identity Erikson in 1964 suggested that identity is the basis of one's being, it involves being authentic to oneself in action, and it correlates to one's understanding of reality. Erikson's view of an identity as being true to oneself in action mirrors in Hart et al.'s (1998) interpretation of moral identity as "a commitment to one's sense of self to lines of action that promote or protect the welfare of others" (p. 515). Research in the field of developmental models of self-identity has implied that identity includes some elements of the ideal self and functions as the ideal principle of action (Blasi, 1984, 1993).

Furthermore, Blasi (1984) argued that a person's moral identities can differ in content. This actually means that one individual may see being merciful as essential to his moral identity, someone else may accentuate being civil and honorable. However, Blasi's (1984) analysis proposes that there is a set moral trait which is likely basic to most individual's moral self-definition. According, Blasi being a moral person is, but not by default, a part of an individual's overall self-definition. This means that being a good or moral person may take up different levels of importance in people's self-concepts.

Rather, the self-importance of an individual's identity and motivational strength may differentiate over time (Hart et al., 1998), and, therefore, his motivational strength. Albeit, the self-importance of individual's moral identity may change, what remains basic to Blasi's view is that when a strong moral identity is not present, the ability to execute intricate moral judgments and present moral arguments is not necessarily a moral behavior. Domination of moral identity in motivating moral conduct was more energetically proclaimed by Damon and Hart (1992), who concluded that "there are both theoretical and empirical reasons to believe centrality of morality to self is the single most powerful determiner of concordance between moral judgment and conduct....People whose self-concept organizes around their moral beliefs are highly likely to translate those beliefs into action consistently throughout their lives" (p. 455).

Identities are the traits and characteristics, social relations, roles, and social group memberships that define who one is. Identities focus on the past or what was once true, the present, what is true at this time, or the future or what the person expects or wishes to become, the person feels obligated to try to become, or the person fears they may become. Identities give a meaning-making lens and focus one's attention on some, but not other features of the immediate context (Oyserman, 2007, 2009a, 2009b). Identities make up one's self-concept variously described as what comes to mind when one thinks of oneself (Neisser, 1993; Stets & Burke, 2003; Stryker, 1980; Tajfcl, 1981), or one's theory of one's personality (Markus & Cross, 1990),

WHEN SELF-IMPORTANCE TAKES PRECEDENCE

Our society is overly selfish and fine with it. Most of people are inconsiderate in general. It is the media and society that propose deceitful dreams. You are not as important as you think you are. Tyler Durden explained it, "You are not a beautiful or unique snowflake, you are the same organic decaying matter as everything else."

The name originates from the phrase "special snowflake", which represents a person who is self-obsessed and delicate, easily insulted, or unable to deal with contending opinions. Many experts conclude that snowflake is "now used as an insult to describe someone who is 'overly sensitive or as feeling entitled to special treatment or consideration'". The word snowflake a while ago had positive connotations and was often used to characterize young adults with a unique personality and potential." "Snowflake" first became popular as slander in the US after the première of 1996 Brad Pitt film Fight Club.

Generation Snowflake is a phrase used to describe the modern generation of hypersensitive millennial. Collins dictionary represents Generation Snowflake as: "The generation of people who became adults in the 2010s, viewed as being less resilient and more prone to taking offense than earlier generations."

Claire Fox, academic and head of the Institute of Ideas think-tank, explains that Snowflake generation has an "almost belligerent sense of entitlement." Fox said: "They assume their emotional suffering takes precedence. Express a view they disagree with and you must immediately recant and apologize."

Howard Schwartz, professor emeritus of Oakland University, has for many years researched the psychology underlying political correctness, and in his book Political Correctness and the Destruction of Social Order: Chronicling the Rise of the Pristine Self, he explains why the term "snowflakes" is now compatible with college students today. Schwartz said the Snowflake originates from what he calls "the rise of the pristine self."

Schwartz explains in his book that "this is a self touched by nothing but love. The problem is that nobody is touched by nothing but love, and so if a person has this as an expectation, if they have built their sense of themselves around this premise, the inevitable appearance of something other than love blows this structure apart." He continues in his interview that "the over-sensitivity of people today, including political correctness and microaggressions, all stem from this idea that people operating under notion of the pristine self view you as evil because you are showing them something other than love."

Schwartz adds "People now experience the entire world as a form of bullying. The helicopter parent protects the children from real dangers, but also fantasy dangers. These precious snowflakes are the children of political correctness, their parents and schools lead them to believe that the world is perfectly moralistic — they don't live in the real world, it is a fantasy,"

According to Schwartz, the pristine self is a type of narcissism or people who regard themselves as pristine selves and cannot handle the unlovingness of the world, even if it manifests itself in indifference and not animosity.

Special Snowflake Syndrome is affecting a significant percentage of the human population wherein the distressed will need special treatment, conduct themselves with a foolish, fabricated sense of entitlement, and in general make the lives of everyone around them miserable. This disease is dangerous by default, because the sufferers don't know they have contracted it, and carry on their enjoyable way under the assumption that other people are the problem.

If you are at some point confronted with an individual that you suspect is harboring Special Snowflake Syndrome, your best course of action is to run away.

KNOW YOURSELF

From the ancient Greek saying "know thyself" to modern psychology, the subject of self-awareness was deliberated by philosophers and psychologists for more than a century.

In this chapter, I will explain what self-awareness is, how it is valuable, why it is hard to achieve, and how one can develop it. Certainly, high self-awareness generally improves an individual and his social relations.

The phrase self-awareness is an awareness of the self, where the self is what makes an individual's identity unique. Identity includes thoughts, experiences, values, and abilities.

Shelley Duval and Robert Wicklund's developed the theory of self-awareness in 1972. According to these psychologists: "when we focus our attention on ourselves, we evaluate and compare our current behavior to our internal standards and values. We become self-conscious as objective evaluators of ourselves." Hence, self-awareness is a considerable mechanism of self-control.

Self-awareness involves monitoring our inner worlds, thoughts, emotions, and beliefs. It is an extensive mechanism influencing personal development that needs self-examination. An honest, non-judgmental self-analysis is a difficult undertaking because we tend to berate ourselves for our failings or fantasize about how great we are when this is not the case. We all have a unique blend of "good" and "bad" attributes, but we are largely ignorant of them. In order to self-reflect objectively, we need to quiet our minds and open our hearts, forgiving ourselves for our imperfections and offering ourselves kudos, but only where we deserve them (T. Davis, 2019).

Self-awareness is having a clear understanding of your personality, including strengths, weaknesses, understandings, thoughts, beliefs, inspirations, and feelings. Self-awareness allows you to understand others, how they see you, your demeanor and your reactions to them. Thus, having awareness generates the opportunity to make changes in behavior and beliefs.

In the best-selling book "Emotional Intelligence," psychologist Daniel Goleman defined self-awareness as "knowing one's internal states, preference, resources, and intuitions."

Although self-awareness concentrates on ourselves it also relates to our understanding of our inner world. According to Goleman self-awareness is a key feature of emotional intelligence.

One must never have any judgment about his thoughts and experiences because an individual must acknowledge and accept himself. Self-awareness allows us to lucidity condition our mind, which can form the foundation of freeing the mind from it.

Being able to oversee our emotions and thoughts from moment to moment is essential to understanding ourselves little better, being satisfied with who we are and proactively directing our thoughts, emotions, and behaviors.

High self-awareness is a strong prognosticator of success in life, perhaps because a self-aware person knows when an opportunity is a good fit for them and how to make the appropriate undertaking work well. Actually, most of us are functioning on "autopilot," barely aware of why we succeed or fail, or why we behave as we do (T. Davis, 2019).

In a study done by Green Peak Partners and Cornell University, 72 executives at public and private companies, participated. The participants had earnings in the range from $50 million to $5 billion, and it was determinate that "a high self-awareness score was a substantial prognosticator of long-term success.

Psychologists Matthew Killingsworth and Daniel T. Gilbert determinate that nearly half of the time we function on "automatic pilot" or unconscious of what we are doing, this happens because our mind strays to somewhere else other than the present moment.

Daniel Kahneman, a Nobel Prize winner for his contribution to behavioral science., explains the difference between the "experiencing self" and the "remembering self," and why this affects our decision-making process.

Kahneman explains that the way we feel about the experience at the moment and way we remember the experience is very different and share only 50% correlation.

This dissimilarity can have a meaningful impact on the account we have of the events, the way we relate to self and other people, and the decisions we make, even though we may not note this dissimilarity often.

Developing self-awareness allows you to make changes in your thoughts and interpretations of reality. Changing your subjective interpretations of reality gives you the opportunity to alter your feelings. It is well-known that self-awareness is one of the principal attributes of Emotional Intelligence and a valuable factor in accomplishing success. Being self-aware about everything is central, and not only being aware of the prevailing emotion one is feeling.

SELF-DECEPTION

People unconsciously prefer rose-colored views of themselves to precise ones. From accidents, failed web sites, businesses and the stock market to industrial disasters and catastrophic wars, the cost of overconfidence is there for all to notice. Even granting that some "positive illusions" could be enticing, is it possible for a rational person to deceive himself into holding them? Certainly, the beneficial consequences of the self—serving beliefs are far from clear: while "thinking positive" is generally viewed as good, self—deception is not, even though the former is only a specific form of the latter (R. Benabou, J. Tirole, 2001).

Individuals may just acquire utility from thinking good about themselves, and conversely, find a bad self-image agonizing. Self-confidence is valuable capital, because believing that one has certain positive characteristics may make it simple to convince everyone else of it. Definitely, confidence in personal abilities and competence can benefit the person and inspire him to undertake more ambitious goals and endure in hardship.

In social interactions and romantic relationships, people prefer self—confident partners compared to self—doubting ones and invest their time and strength in supporting partner's intentions.

According, motivation theory people have incomplete knowledge of their own performances, or more generally of the concluding costs and consequences of their actions. Additionally, ability and effort influence determining performance; in most instances, they are complements, so that a higher self-confidence improves the motivation to act.

Standard observation is that morale has a key role in difficult endeavors, nonetheless, it is when people expect to fail that they manage to fail effectively, and failure leads to disappointment more rapidly for people with low self-esteem (Salancik, 1977).

Some people are suffering from time inconsistency (e.g., hyperbolic discounting), the present self has the interest to develop the self-confidence of future selves, as the self helps to oppose their natural tendency to quit too easily. People consciously are ignorant of their personal abilities, and so they deliberately hinder their own performance or choose tasks in which they are highly likely to fail.

There is a less rational side of human inference which is determinate through research that people are likely to recall their successes more often than their failures, and have self-serving biased recollections and interpretations of their past accomplishments. Some people have the inclination to overestimate their abilities and positive characteristics, as well as their influence on the overall situation. Additionally, this leads them to optimism about future events in their life, and look upon negatively on possible unfortunate events and outcomes.

According to Heider (1958), there is a distinction between temporary (situational) and enduring (dispositional) characteristics. In the social comparison process (Festinger, 1954), individuals assess their ability by comparing their performance with that of people facing similar circumstances and conditions. They are actually using "relative performance evaluation", or "benchmarking", for self-evaluation. A good estimation of performance by others is hereby harmful to an individual's self-esteem, and conversely, some comfort derives when others face adversity. A person interprets praise and criticism taking into account not only what the others say or do, but also their intentions in the social context.

Nowadays, all over the world, self—confidence is generally regarded as a valuable personal asset. Going back at least to William James, an important branch of psychology has advocated "believing in oneself" as a key feature to achieving success. Self—help industry is flourishing, a large part of it is encouraging people to improve their self—esteem shed "helplessness" and reap the awards of "positivity".

The question which instantly comes to mind is: why is a positive view of oneself, as opposed to a completely authentic one, seen as such a good thing to have? The answer is that when one thinks of himself favorably it makes them happier. High self-confidence may propel people to undertake activities that are risky and that they would not usually do. When one believes in his over average abilities or integrity it is easier for him to convince other people that he posses such abilities. Thus, to lie most convincingly one must trust his own lies.

The correlation between self—confidence, and motivation was discussed in the psychology literature, from early writers like James (1890) to contemporary ones like Bandura (1977). Self-handicapping is an intriguing phenomenon when people deliberately create obstacles to their own performance. Hence, people set themselves overambitious objectives, where they will most definitely fail. Indeed, people obviously self-handicap more in public situations (Kolditz and Arkin (1982)). Interestingly enough, psychologists have not reached a definite conclusion on whether high or low self-confidence people are the most defensive of their egos, although there does seem to be evidence in favor of the first assumption.

Thus Greenier et al. (1995) explain "humanistically oriented theories, ... according to which high self-esteem people's feelings of self-worth are built on solid foundations that do not need continual validation", with experimental research determinate that "high self-esteem people are the more likely to display self-serving attributions, self-handicap to enhance the potentially positive implications of good performance, set inappropriately risky goals when ego-threatened, and actively create less fortunate others with whom they can compare favorably."

Self—handicapping may help a time-inconsistent individual secure his motivation. In the framework of hedonic beliefs, workers in a hazardous job may not want to know about the exact risks involved with the job (Akerlof and Dickens, 1982).

How to deal with the bad news about one's accomplishments and abilities that life surely brings. There are psychological memory instruments of defensive denial, oppression, constraint, self—serving attributions and so on.

Psychologists and philosophers have researched for a long time people's common tendency to deny, withhold, revoke, and selectively remember information that threatens their ego.

Freudian repression is the most obvious example, but various other forms of provoked cognition and self—deception feature greatly in modern psychology. Hence, the research has confirmed that people tend to recall their successes more than their failures (e.g., Korner (1950), Mischel et al. (1976)), have self—serving tendentious recollections of their past performances (Crary (1996)), and readily find "evidence" in their personal histories that they have aspects which they view (sometimes as the result of experimental manipulation) as correlated with success in professional or personal life (Kunda and Sanitioso (1989), Murray and Holmes (1993)). Conversely, they often engage in "beneffactance", viewing themselves as instrumental for good, but not bad outcomes (Zuckerman (1979)). When they commit a bad deed they revaluate the facts and try to assure themselves that it was not as bad ("he deserved it", "the damage was limited"), or associate the responsibility to others (Snyder (1985)).

Gur and Sackeim (1979) concluded that self—deception as a situation in which: a) the person holds two contradictory beliefs; b) he is not aware of holding one of the beliefs; c) this lack of awareness is motivated. Conversely, receiving positive feedback triggers a cue-based "warm glow" effect, which automatically makes accessible to the person other instances of himself in positive circumstances (Greenwald, 1980).

As already explained, audits, experiments, and day-to-day observation consistently suggest that most people overestimate their past accomplishments, abilities and other desirable traits, both in absolute terms and relative to other people (Weinstein (1980), Taylor and Brown (1988)), also reflective people don't appear like an exception. A survey of college professors determinates that 94% of them thought they were better than their average colleague (Gilovich, (1991)). This demonstrates common irrationality in human assumption.

SELF-CONFIDENCE

"**M**ost people live in a restricted circle of potential."

This statement of William James holds no less true today than when he made it over a century ago. The reason that so many people never fulfill their potential is not a lack of intelligence, opportunities or resources, but a lack of trust in themselves. Or put another way, too little self-confidence. Without it, you can do little, with it, you can do anything (M. Warrell, 2015)!

The Cambridge Dictionary defines self-confidence as "the quality of being certain of your abilities or of having trust in people, plans, or the future". It's a positive quality that every person wants to have.

A definition provided by Branden (1994) describes self-esteem as confidence in our ability to determinate and cope with the essential challenges of life. Deep trust in our right of being successful and happy, the feeling of being worthy, deserving, entitled to affirm our needs and wants and achieve our principles. Furthermore, confidence is part of the connotation of self-esteem and at the same time, self-esteem is an important aspect in the development of confidence. Dörnyei (2005) indicated that the concept of self-confidence relates to self-esteem and both share a familiar emphasis on the individual's perception of his or her abilities as a human.

There are many definitions of self-confidence, Glenda and Anstey (1990) concluded that many phrases such as self-evaluation, self-satisfaction, self-appraisal, and self-confidence are interchangeable. John and Srivastava (1999) relate self-confidence to the Big Five personality dimensions of extraversion, which, involve an energetic focus toward the social and material world, sociability and positive emotionalism that is projected.

Glenda and Anstey (1990), Pierce et al. (1989), Brockner (1988) and Bandura (1982) specified that some factors that build general self-confidence derive from several features. The most important of which are: 1) common personal experiences; positive experiences increase self-confidence, while the negative experiences have the opposite effect and 2) social and friendly messages received from other people with authority, such as school community, associates and family are important for self-confidence enhancement. Sharing positive communication with others is detrimental to the development of high self-confidence, although, exposure to negative communication decreases the level of self-confidence of the individual.

Krashen (1985) believed that since a person, in general, has imperfect knowledge of his personal abilities, people who acquire benefits from his performance (parent, spouse, friend, teacher, manager, etc.) have a motivation to manipulate his self–confidence (R. Bénabou J. Tirole, 2000).

The first premise of our analysis is that people have imperfect knowledge of their own abilities in many of the tasks they face. Second, we adopt a cognitive approach, assuming that the person is an information processor who extracts from his environment signals that are relevant for his self–confidence.

According to Deci (1975, p. 41): If a person's feelings of competence and self–determination are enlarged, his intrinsic motivation will increase. If his feelings of competence and self–determination are diminished, his intrinsic motivation will decrease. Some rewards or feedback will increase intrinsic motivation through this process and others will decrease it, either through this process or through the change in the perceived arrangement of causality.

The base for formation of self-confidence is an adequate behavioral collection, the affirmative knowledge in resolving social problems and success in reaching a person's own goals. Conclusive subjective evaluation of the effects of the person's actions and evaluations, which acknowledge other's opinion that is respected by the person is also valuable to form self-confidence in comparison with commonly accepted standards of success, prominence, property, financial and social status, capital, etc.. The positive assessment of the opportunity, quality, and efficiency of person's talents, experience, and capabilities are deciding factor of social courage in setting new objectives and assignments, as well as motivation of the person to achieve his goals.

Overconfidence decreases fear and can lead to outcomes that are uncertain about their end results. A confident person is likely to overlook the real risks and disregard the real danger. Thus, a high level of self-confidence may influence even perception of one's health (overly confident people can assume that they can, smoke cigarettes and abuse alcohol, or drugs and there are will not be any ramifications). Overconfident people all too often create and nourish unrealistic expectations.

A person, who behaves confidently, is self-determinate, speaks with certainty and loudly. He demands what desires, expresses his feelings and often uses the word "I". Also, the confidant person is assertive in a relaxed manner.

When a person lacks self-confidence, they are quiet and uncertain. Often they explain themselves unnecessary, are impersonal, keeping a low profile, and afraid to ask or demand even things that are rightfully theirs.

Self-knowledge on self-presentation, influence the correlation between the "inner self" and the "outer self". Confident self-presentation is defined as presenting an individual's self-esteem in social situations. There is extensive literature in social psychology which addresses the issue of self-presentation, mainly behaviors and attitudes (self-promotion, justification, invocation, intimidation, ingratiation, etc.) that are critical and aim at manipulating other individual's opinions about oneself. For example, Baumeister (1998) characterizes self-presentation as "attempts to convey information about or images of oneself to others". This topic has also been widely explored in economics, although with very different range of applications, under the caption of signaling theory (Spence 1974).

Depression has a long history of being diagnosed as a disorder of self-esteem (Bibring 1953, Freud 1957). Its symptoms in psychology are poor self-image, inhibition of all activity, public acceptance of an individual's weaknesses, lack of interest in the external world, low tolerance for disappointment, etc. Of particular interest in our analysis are the self-esteem maintenance and self-presentation approaches used by depressed people to endure their situation.

Depressed people need and thus seek others' attention sometimes. They have a major interest to confirm they are worthy and loved, it is the reason why they are searching for compassion and reassurance (Cohen 1954, Coyne 1976). Nonetheless, they are often unreceptive to the positive feedback which others may offer to them (Hill et al. 1986). Also, they are willing to bring upon themselves disapproval to avoid requests to perform. It is, through acts and words, that they confess their weakness in so they can ask for leniency on a set of obligations, and attempt to lower others' standards or expectancies (Shaw 1982, Hill et al. 1986).

Psychologists, prominent scientists in human resource management and sociologists have underlined for a while now, the critical role played by self-esteem and self-perception in the personal initiative, motivation and social relations. People are able to make conclusions about their selves from others' behavior and to evaluate the influence of their own actions on others' feelings.

New research into neural plasticity shows that we can completely rewire our brains in manners that alter our opinions and behavior at any time. This implies that it doesn't matter how shy or doubtful you've been up to now, you can build your self-confidence voluntarily. Certainly, it necessitates constant dedication, effort, and the openness to take worthwhile risks. Also, one must never rely on external affirmation to confirm and sustain his worth, rather act as he already has the self-confidence he aspires to have because confidence itself is dependent from the way others perceive us.

Alex Malley, bestselling author of The Naked CEO said, "The only way to build self-confidence is to take a risk and take action despite your fear of failure, messing up or embarrassment. If things work out, then you now know you can do more than you think. If things don't work out, you now know that you can handle more than you think. Either way, you're better off." Conversely, it is out of the comfort zone where self-confidence rises.

Studies have determinate that women are not likely to start a new task unless they feel certain that they can carry it out successfully, in contrast, men are likely to take even long-shot risks.

SELF-PRESENTATION

Everybody tries to control the impressions that he or she makes on others. This is known as self-presentation. According to Leary, it is the process by which people convey to other people that they are specific kind of person or have specific characteristics (Leary 1996:17). In this perspective, self-presentation is a type of impression management of others' impressions in a social context (Leary,1993). Self-presentation is either conscious or unconscious. It has significance for the smooth functioning of social relations (Leary, 1996).

Self-presentation is a complicated issue in social psychology. Self-presentations become influential by default, especially when people want to do something, such as improving or initiating relationships, doing well on a job interview or obtaining sympathy. It is important for aiding communication that we take care of how we look, smell and act. Usually, "our behavior is [...] constrained by our concerns with others' impressions" (Leary, 1996: 3). If it is not constrained, we can find ourselves in an uncomfortable situation.

One of the reasons why self-presentation on social networking sites is somewhat different from face-to-face is that the online one is inspected, edited and revised (Walther, Slovacek & Tidwell, 2001: 110).

Furthermore, with the exchange of characteristic features of culture and identity on the Internet, and especially on social networking sites, it is possible that online self-presentation influences offline identity formation (Kosanovic, 2006). Furthermore, young adults seem to socialize regularly and intimately on the Internet (Birnie & Horvath, 2002), and the process of identity formation is going on in adolescence (Hogg & Vaughan, 2006), we could claim, today young people's self-concept forms on the internet, especially in the cases where people invent and build an ideal self and not a realistic self. And most of the population, often present ideal sides of ourselves in social interaction (S. Zarghooni, 2007).

Self-description is plainly how people self-present using words. These descriptions present something about an individual's values, political or religious affiliation, likes or dislikes, occupation, or accomplishments in life (Leary, 1996). Those who want to make certain self-presentation will oversee their self-description carefully because self-description is a basic feature of impression management. According to Leary people do not lie a lot when self-describing, rather they "are more likely to selectively present true information about themselves" (Learey, 1996: 18).

According to Leary, emotions are not just internal but are also communicated to others (Leary, 1996). Through emotion expressions, we can guide other's impressions of us. When people are angry they generally show it apparently (Leary, 1996). Monitoring an individual's emotional expressions is a tool of influential self-presentation. Basically, Leary concluded that "far from being spontaneous expressions of feelings, emotional expressions can serve as self-presentation" (Leary, 1996: 24)

Physical appearance has a powerful effect on others' impressions of us. Physically attractive people are "perceived as more sociable, dominant, intelligent, socially skilled, and adjusted" (Feingold, 1992, in Leary, 1996: 25). Additionally, it is "perhaps the clearest nonverbal channel of self-expression". Thus, physical appearance is very important for self-presentation. Others consider being attractive as positive, and a lot of positive attributes relate to physical attractiveness. It is understandable that various groups have different standards for what is attractive, Leary concludes that whatever we do with our appearance is self-presentational (Leary, 1996). Actions that influence ones' self-presentation are both conscious and non-conscious.

There is a self-presentational method related to social associations. This indirect method relates to people who do not emphasize their own personal attributes, rather they promote their connections with acclaimed or successful social entities, such as sports teams, celebrities or other popular artists. In this instance, they take part in some of these units' positive relations. Its name is BIRGing, or "basking in reflected glory" (Forsyth, 2002: 94)

Leary indicates that embarrassing situations are "self-presentational predicaments", which are "[e]vents that clearly (and, sometimes, irrevocably) damage a person's image in others' eyes" (Leary, 1996:118). Furthermore, these embarrassing events contrast the impression that one has constructed. Miller distinguishes between several types of predicaments, those caused by ones' actions and those that can happen during direct interaction with others (Miller, 1992, in Leary, 1996).

Individuals want to present themselves in a positive way. Paradoxically, the fear of looking too pretentious may lead people to modesty and the self-presentation becomes unsuccessful (S. Zarghooni, 2007). One of the most important images people want to project to the world is likeability and competence.

SELF-EXPRESSION

"The journey of self-discovery is the most important journey we can take" (De la Huerta, 2014).

The right to freedom of expression is the right of a person entirely in his capacity as an individual. It derives from the widely accepted premise of Western thought that the proper end of man is a comprehension of his character and potentialities as a human person (Thomas Emerson, 1963).

The way we present and express ourselves to other people forms the core of our personality, as understood by everyone but us, and sets the path our life is taking. It's a crucial aspect of life to give attention to, especially if you want to feel understood and more in tune with others (C. Ackermam, 2018).

"We define self-expression as expressing one's thoughts and feelings, and these expressions are accomplished through words, choices or actions." (Kim & Ko, 2007).

Kim and Ko (2007) conclude that self-expression is one of the most highly regarded and venerated values in Western civilization because of the near-deification of "the individual" in our society. Furthermore, self-expression a crucial practice of Western culture, it is also nestled into the fundamentals of psychology. Psychology is studying the mind, including the self, others, and groups of people. We acquire knowledge about the mind through an expression of individuals—verbally or otherwise (Kim & Ko, 2007).

While those of us in the West have embraced individualistic norms and practices, including self-expression, other cultures have upheld collectivist values and—in some cases—placed little to no value on individualism. For instance, the Arab world is less prone to individualistic views and more likely to value tradition, religion, and authority (Inglehart et al., 2014).

In general, psychological conclusions support the concept that self-expression affects people in a positive way (e.g., Freud, 1920/1966; Pennebaker, 1990).

However, various studies in cultural psychology conclude that the concept of self varies to the extent that the meaning of the self differs, how people engage in particular self-actions, such as self-expression, and their psychological ramifications could vary as well. The way human beings express themselves and the way different forms of expression influence people differ depending on the presumptions about the self and its relation in a given social situation.

Self-expression is expressing persons' thoughts and feelings, expressed by words, choices or actions. Furthermore, western culture has defined the person as superior (Markus & Kitayama, 1991; Triandis, 1989). Rousseau believed that man in his purest state was free of the sediments of society (Rousseau, 1750/1997).

Self-expression allows people to differentiate themselves from others, to present their own opinions and desires, and substantiate their personal self-concepts.

Extensive research on choice behaviors has concluded that people try to show and enlarge the presentation of individuality, autonomy, and self-empowerment in their choices (Belk, 1988; Han & Shavitt, 1994). Additionally, studies determine that people show their self-identities through their choices and preferences for objects and opinions (Prentice, 1987; Smith, Bruner, &

White, 1956).

Individuals favor possessions, attitudes, and values that embody their personal-identity (Prentice, 1987), and seek to differentiate from others to affirm and present their own uniqueness (Ratner & Kahn, 2002; Snyder & Fromkin, 1977). Belk (1988) believed that it is a reflection of self through his personal choices that allows him to extend his self to possessions.

Freud was confident that only through verbal expression could an individual really gain perspective into his own psyche (Breuer & Freud, 1957). Suppression of self-expression relates to mental illness and psychopathology (Freud, 1923/1961; Pennebaker & Beall, 1986). Emphasis on expression is a fundamental aspect of individualism (Bellah, Madsen, Sullivan, Swidler, & Tipton, 1985). People in individualist cultural concepts are prone to self-express since it involves asserting "a unique core of feeling and intuition (Bellah et al., 1985, p. 334)"

Speech is a representative form of self-expression, it holds particular importance in the Western cultural concepts as elementary means to express one's personal attributes, as "speaking one's mind" is possibly the most effective method to express one's thoughts (Kim & Markus, 2002; Kim & Sherman, 2005). Together with the freedom of choice, freedom of speech embodies an individual's ultimate freedom.

SELF-PROMOTION

Self-promotion is attempting to present oneself to other people as an accomplished, capable, intelligent and talented person. Self-promotion is done through face-to-face conversation, on blogs or social media, in public appearances, or even through our mannerisms, posture, conversation or clothing. Self-promotion is a common tendency as we wish for others to perceive us as possessing admirable qualities.

As explained self-promotion indicates the habit to consciously present oneself as very competent to others. When it comes to self-promoting people, the basic intention is seen by others as proficient, intelligent, or skilled. Self-promotion has various advantageous, especially in a competitive environment. Various studies have determinate methods used by people who try to self-promote. Often people self-promote by referring to oneself in complimentary terms.

People use tactics to self-promote such as leading the conversation to where it is proper to speak about their earlier accomplishments, or in contrast refrain from topics in which others are specialists. Additionally, people try to provide favorable circumstances for others to promote them. However, social networks had become one of the main platforms for self-promotion.

Extensive research concluded that self-promotion can easily

backfire in terms of social likability, but it comes across as boastful and obnoxious to others. People who self-promote tend to believe that others will respond to their self-promotion in a favorable way. Yet, research studies have found the opposite is true. Although self-promotion may make the braggart seem more competent, skillful, intelligent and successful, it usually makes them less likable. Self-promotion can make people come across as conceited and annoying to others. In fact, the more people try to make others like them through methods of self-promotion, the more likely others will dislike them.

During self-promotion, people have an obstacle, because the perception of them is deceptive. Even though the essential feature of self-promotion is for a person to present himself as competent, circumstances must appear when self-promotion will combine with appealing.

Studies have concluded that for women who self-promote perception is less favorable than men who do the same thing. Probably this is due to gender bias where the roles of women conception are being submissive and inactive, in contrast to man.

Supportive research on this issue determinate that women are indecisive when it comes to personal promotion.

Psychology scientists I. Scopelliti, G. Loewenstein, and J. Vosgerau researched why a lot of people often get misunderstood when self-promoting. They concluded that people who self-promote overestimate the emotions their self-promotion elicits and underestimate negative emotions it elicits. Consequently, when people try to influence the thoughts other people have of them, they excessively self-promote, which has the opposite result from the intended one, leaving them as being less likable and as a braggart.

Loewenstein, professor of Economics and Psychology said: "Bragging is probably just the tip of the iceberg of the self-destructive things we do in the service of self-promotion, from unfortunate flourishes in public speeches to inept efforts to 'dress for success' to obviously insincere attempts to ingratiate ourselves to those in power."

"It may be beneficial for people who plan to engage in self-promotion to try to realize that others may actually be less happy than they think to hear about their latest achievement. Recipients of such self-promotion who find themselves annoyed might likewise try to bolster their tolerance in the knowledge that braggarts genuinely underestimate others' negative reactions to their bragging," said Vosgerau, professor of marketing.

SELF-ENHANCEMENT

According to social cognition, self-enhancement means to pursue, control, or boost positivity of self-views above what psychological standards would need. In this manner, social behavior motivation is by default.

The phenomenon of self-enhancement is the motive to pursue, preserve, or augment the positivity of individual's self-views, more so than unprejudiced benchmarks.

Self-protection and self-enhancement most often run in tandem (Alicke & Sedikides, 2009; Sedikides & Gregg, 2008).

Many people self-enhance in many circumstances, they seek, interpret, or falsify evidence about themselves in a way intended to develop, maintain, or amplify a positive self-image. Self-enhancement is a cognitive activity done to enhance beliefs that an individual is a lovable and accomplished person.

It is through the construction of self-favoring narratives, people help themselves to keep up an ideal level of positive emotions as a function (Alicke & Sedikides, 2018) named "psychological housekeeping."

People contribute to the improvement and protection of psychological interests or aims, be it concrete (e.g., talents and abilities like intelligence, athleticism, and musicality) or abstract (like popularity, social status, or security;)(Alicke & Sedikides, 2009;

O'Mara & Gaertner, 2017).

Gebauer, Wagner, Sedikides, and Neberich (2013) imply that "self-centrality breeds self-enhancement,".

The motivational hypothesis states that people strive to feel good about themselves and that nudging their self-other comparisons toward a positive outcome is the way forward to satisfy this desire (Alicke & Govorun, 2005).

Self-improvement indicates the motive of person to become a better person in general, instead, self-enhancement indicates the motive to create the perception that the individual is a competent and accomplished person, regardless if it is true or not.

People who self-enhance are regularly claiming above average strengths and achievements. Self-enhancement is like self-presentation where the person is developing a positive self-image to convince others that he is competent, regardless of personal opinions about one's self. Additionally, people use a range of categorizations to interpret their successes and narrow ones describing their failures.

This is because people arrive at self-serving conclusions about the reasons for their successes and failures. Successful people make personal attributions, hence enlarging their self-images as an accomplished person. In contrast, people who often fail make external attributions and blame the failure on their bad luck, and circumstances, so they are avoiding to admit personal shortcomings. The same principle applies to the acceptance of good news which is taken at face value, on contrast bad news are held to a higher standard and analyzed more closely.

Interestingly, contemporary research suggests that people are tendentious and hold positive views of themselves that are not true. Individuals on average believe that they are anything but average. For example, ordinary human being believes that he is more methodical, socially accepted, visionary, valuable and moral than the average person, but this, of course, is not possible. However, an average person is not above average, because of the logic of statistics.

Individuals also tend to believe that they incline to accomplish positive results and not likely to face unpleasant ones than are other people. It is statistically not realistic for the average person to be more likely to accomplish good results and avoid bad ones.

When foreseeing the future, people overestimate the chance that they will take enticing actions and achieve desired results.

SELF-STEREOTYPING

A stereotype is "...a fixed, over-generalized belief about a particular group or class of people." (Cardwell, 1996).

The advantage of a stereotype is that it allows us to respond quickly to a situation because we may have had a similar previous experience.

Self-stereotyping means perceiving oneself as a part of a group and so behaving appropriately to this social identity (Hardie & McMurray, 1992; Lau, 1989; Lorenzi, Cioldi, 1991; Simon, Glissner-Bayed, & Stratenwerth, 1991; Simon & Hamilton, 1994; Turner, Hogg, Oakes, Reicher, & Wetherell, 1987). Turner (1987) explained that the course of self-categorization provides the fundament for self-stereotyping: self-categorization can lead to a stereotypical self-perception by the person and depersonalization, and then to the expression of in-group normative behavior.

Self-stereotyping is a phenomenon by which people who are members to a stigmatized social group have a tendency to describe themselves in the lines of the stereotypical traits, and not with traits unimportant to the in-group stereotype (M. Latrofa, J. Vaes, M. Cadinu, 2012).

According to social identity theory (Tajfel, 1982; Tajfel & Turner, 1979, 1986; Turner, 1982), which formed the basis for self-categorization theory, human beings try to build positive self-concepts. Affirmative self-concepts encompass two separate components: personal identity (based on specific features person possesses) and social identity (based on association to social groups or collectives (Crocker & Luhtanen, 1990; Luhtanen & Crocker, 1992).

Furthermore, self-stereotyping happens "on all and any dimensions which are believed to be correlated with "a categorization (Hogg & Abrams, 1988), the process can also include the assumption of negative features. In this instance, acceptance of negative stereotypes may, therefore, contribute against the universal human goal of self-enhancement (e.g., Baumeister, 1982; Deaux & Major, 1987; Srull & Wyer, 1989; Swann, 1990; Swann, Stein-Seroussi, & Giesler, 1992; Taylor & Brown, 1989), but rejection of negative stereotypes serves as a denial of valuable social identity (Lorenzi, Cioldi, 1991).

Self-stereotyping happens when individuals' beliefs about their own characteristics are compatible with the general beliefs of the public about the characteristics of a group they belong to. It can negatively influence self-esteem, because members of a group may have stereotypic opinions about the group and themselves. This can also be the case when the behaviors of members of the group are consistent with the stereotypes related to their group.

The positive side of self-stereotyping is that it can create a sense of group unity and acceptance. The closer members feel to the group, the more probable they are to see themselves as possessing characteristics related to the group. In contrast, when group members are slightly different from other members of the group, they will self-stereotype to reduce this feeling. If the group is under threat self-stereotyping among members will increase.

According, social psychology there is a beneficial correlation between the way people speak about themselves and how they speak about their social groups.

SELF-DISCREPANCY

This chapter presents a theory of how various types of discrepancies between self-state representations relate to various type of emotional vulnerabilities. The self-state representation represents one domain of the self (real; ideal; ought) and one standpoint on the self (own; others). It suggests that various types of self-discrepancies represent various types of negative psychological contexts that relate to various types of discomfort.

Discrepancies between the real/own self-state, or the self-concept and ideal self-states are representations of the personal beliefs about own or others' hopes, wishes, or aspirations for the person about negative outcomes, associated with depression-related emotions like disappointment, dissatisfaction, and sadness. In contrast, discrepancies between the real/own self-state and ought self-states, represent an individual's beliefs about his or her own or a significant other's beliefs about the individual's duties, responsibilities, or obligations, that signify the presence of negative outcomes, associated with agitation-related emotions like fear, threat, restlessness. Differences in both the relative size and accessibility of individuals' available types of self-discrepancies relate to differences in the kinds of discomfort people are likely to experience (E.T.Higgins, 1987).

The assumption that people who hold conflicting or unsuitable beliefs are likely to experience discomfort is not new in psychology. Furthermore, in social psychology, there are multiple early theories that propose a relation between discomfort and specific types of "inconsistency" among a person's beliefs (e.g., Abelson & Rosenberg, 1958; Festinger, 1957; Heider, 1958; McGuire, 1968; Newcomb, 1968; Osgood & Tannenbaum, 1955). And there are many classic theories that relate self and affect the proposed that self-conflicts or self-inconsistencies produce emotional problems (e.g., Adler, 1964; Allport, 1955; Cooley, 1902/1964; Freud, 1923/1961; Homey, 1939, 1946; James, 1890/1948; Lecky, 1961; Mead, 1934; Rogers, 1961).

The self-discrepancy theory has the following aims: (a) to differentiate various types of discomfort that people holding unsuitable beliefs may experience, and (b) to relate multiple types of emotional vulnerabilities systematically to various types of discrepancies that people may have as self-beliefs.

Various types of belief incompatibility is defined in the literature, for instance, dissonance (e.g., Aronson, 1969; Festinger, 1957), imbalance (e.g., Heider, 1958; Newcomb, 1968), incongruity (e.g., Osgood & Tannenbaum, 1955), and self-inconsistency (e.g., Epstein, 1980; Lecky, 1961). However, the emotional consequences of this incompatibility description are tension, unpleasantness, burden, adversity, irritation, conflict, stress, or discomfort.

Basic purpose of self-discrepancy theory is to determinate which types of incompatible beliefs will cause which types of negative emotions. One more purpose is to contemplate whether the availability and accessibility of various types of incompatible beliefs cause various types of irritation. Incompatible beliefs are cognitive constructs, and they vary in their availability and their accessibility. Construct availability refers to specific types of constructs that are available in memory used to process current information, whereas construct accessibility refers to the readiness with which each separately stored construct is processed (Higgins & Bargh, 1987; Higgins, King, & Mavin,

1982; Tulving & Pearlstone, 1966). Personal differences can appear either because people have different types of constructs available or because they have the same constructs but their subjective accessibility differentiate (E.T.Higgins, 1987).

Extensive evidence shows that different contextual factors, for instance, earlier exposure to stimuli, can induce brief personal differences of accessibility of universally available social constructs (e.g., "inflexible" or "averse") and these differences can originate differences in the consecutive responses to social stimuli (Higgins, Bargh, & Lombardi, 1985; Higgins & King, 1981; Wyer- & Srull, 1981).

There is also proof that constant personal differences in construct accessibility can influence social information processing (e.g., Bargh & Thein, 1985; Gotlib & McCann, 1984; Higgins et al., 1982). The self-discrepancy theory has also purpose to present construct accessibility as a predictor of available types of incompatible beliefs that can induce discomfort.

In self-discrepancy theory, there are multiple features of the self or self-images. One facet has descriptions of two "real" selves, the type of person one believes he or she is and the type of person an individual believes that others think he or she actually is. The "others" are the significant others or the universal others (see Erikson, 1950/1963; Lecky, 1961; Mead, 1934; Wylie, 1979). In addition to the described real selves, an array of different possible selves emerges (e.g., Markus & Nurius, 1987). James (1890/1948), For instance, the "spiritual" self, that includes one's own moral sense and conscience, and the "social" self, that includes the self that is worthy of being approved by the highest social merit. Rogers (1961) differentiates between normative standard or what other people believe a person should or ought to be and an individual's personal belief about what he or she would "ideally" like to be.

Various self-state representations relate to three fundamental domains of the self (a) the real self, which is your representation of the attributes that someone (yourself or others) believes you actually have; (b) the ideal self, which is your representation of the attributes that someone (yourself or another) would like you, ideally, get (i.e., representation of someone's expectations, ambitions, or wishes for you); and (c) the ought self, which is your representation of the attributes that someone (yourself or another) believes you should or ought to get (i.e., representation of someone's sense of your commitment, obligations, accountability or responsibilities).

There is the distinction between the ideal self and the ought self presented in different distinctions proposed in the literature (e.g., Colby, 1968; James, 1890/1948; Piers & Singer, 1971; Rogers, 1961; Schafer, 1967).

Connecting the domains of the self with every standpoint of the self forms six basic types of self-state representations: real/own, real/other, ideal/own, ideal/other, ought/own, and ought/other. The first two self-state representations (especially real/own) constitute what is typically meant by an individual's self-concept (see Wylie, 1979). The four remaining self-state representations are self-directive standards or obtained guides for the self (Higgins, Strauman, & Klein, 1986). The self-discrepancy theory proposes that people vary as to which self-guide they are especially motivated to meet. Not all people possess all the self-guides, because some people may possess only ought self-guides, nonetheless, others may possess only ideal self-guides. The self-discrepancy theory hypothesizes that people's motivation reaches a condition where our self-concept matches our personally relevant self-guides (E.T.Higgins, 1987).

Self-discrepancy theory suggests that personal differences in types of self-discrepancies associated with differences in the specific types of negative psychological situations their possessors are experiencing.

SOCIAL COMPARISON

Social comparison theory was first suggested in 1954 by psychologist Leon Festinger who explained that people have an internal drive to evaluate themselves, usually in comparison to others. Certainly, people make different judgments about themselves, and one of the basic manners that we do this is through social comparison, or appraising the self with others.

Social comparison is a crucial psychological phenomenon essential to comprehending both social behavior and development of identity. People look to similar others to evaluate their personal abilities and beliefs. Looking up to those superior to oneself for inspiration and advice can help to gather information about social norms and hints about how to act, also to experience emotions for other people based on a correlation of mutual differences. Individuals compare with others to gather self-knowledge, to self-improve, to self-enhance, protect themselves, to achieve positive self-image, to self-motivate, to decrease the uncertainty, and connect socially with others.

Even though enthusiasm in social comparison phenomena has waned over the years, Festinger's (1954a, 1954b) theory of social comparison processes has remained the most influential conceptual framework to accompany this area of study (Goethals, 1986).

Fundamental features of Festinger's original concept have remained unchanged, noticeably that (1) another person's similarity to oneself is a crucial criterion for social comparison; (2) existence of tendencies toward social comparison, and (3) the processes of social comparison differentiates across concept domains of comparison. For instance, a "unidirectional drive to do better and better" exists when comparing one's abilities but not one's opinions (Festinger, 1954a), and a preference for similar others is more noticeable in the domain of values than that of thoughts (Goethals & Darley, 1977). There are two types of social comparisons, upward and downward social comparisons, which by default are judgemental processes of comparative judgments.

Contextual dependence of motivationally compatible information is Tesser's (1988) research on self-esteem development. Furthermore, Festinger (1954a) concluded that regarding their abilities, people are satisfied only by knowing that she or he outperformed similar others, Tesser (1989) in case only for abilities important to the self-concept.

As already explained, social comparison plays an important role in the judgments people make about themselves but also in the way people act in different circumstances. Occasionally some comparisons might influence the person to feel incompetent, while other comparisons originate confidence and help improve self-esteem. As one compares himself to others, he must consider how both upward and downward social comparison may influence his thoughts, confidence, inspiration, attitude, and character. Also, be aware we incline to make biased comparisons, thus negative feelings might emerge as a result of an upward social comparison, or superior attitudes result from downward social comparison.

Research is done by S. Deri, S. Davidai, and T. Gilovich that analyzed the factors that may govern FOMO (the "fear of missing out") and the feeling that other people have better social lives than us. The researchers concluded that people believe that they spend more time by themselves, go to fewer gatherings, and are part of fewer social groups than others, including their closest

friends. Nonetheless, these researchers discovered that this oc-
curred partly because people compared themselves to highly dis-
tinguishable, and highly social people.

ILLUSION OF CONTROL

The Illusion of Control was first identified by Ellen Langer in 1975 in her research paper "The Illusion of Control" published in The Journal of Personality and Social Psychology.

The illusion of control is the cognitive bias represented by the tendency of human beings to believe they can control or at least influence outcomes that they actually have no influence over.

Langer concluded that people often behave as if chance events are controllable. Through a series of experiments, Langer showed a predominance of the illusion of control and that people were more likely to act as if they could exercise control in a luck situation where 'skill cues' were present.

By skill cues, Langer meant features of the situation correlated with the exercise of skill, especially the exercise of choice, competition, familiarity with the conditions and involvement in decision-making.

Further research has demonstrated that even though intelligent, knowledgeable, and reasonable, people regularly believe they have control over events in their lives, even though such control is not realistic.

Surprisingly, later research determinate that although most people operate under the illusion of control at least partly, depressed people are not likely to have these illusions. Depressed people actually have a better understanding of reality especially when it comes to accurately assess control, and are less susceptible to illusions.

There are ideal situations in life where we have complete control of the outcome. These rare situations allow us to glow and demonstrate our hard labor and our strengths.

Individuals often embellish their ability to deliver the desired outcome. Even when it comes to controlling chance events, people are confident they are in control.

However, people do not overestimate their control in every situation. There are conceptual factors and attributes of the people involved that are both crucial.

Studies have demonstrated people believe that they have better control over the outcome of a game with dice if they throw the dice themselves and not if someone else throws the dice for them, presumably because people assume better odds of winning because they throw the dice.

Additional research has examined the origins of the illusion of control since originally, researchers concluded that people confuse chance and skill because situations favorable to an illusion of control are often similar to situations where people show their skills. The illusion of control, then, might result from the continual correlation of one's own behavior in a situation with the desired outcome. Most of the time this correlation is correct, nonetheless, sometimes it is not, as in situations where the outcome happens randomly.

Individuals who feel they don't have control over situations may develop a state of learned helplessness, and take foolish and unnecessary risks. In contrast, when people see they are in control it may lead them to experience positive feelings and try new, more challenging tasks. This all depends on situational and personal factors.

The biggest difficulty with the phenomenon illusion of control is that it can lead to frustration and occasionally anger. Individuals blaming their selves for outcomes that aren't their fault. This is particularly true when the stakes are high.

If a person is putting in as much effort as one can and is taking all the precautions within his control to influence the desired outcome he has done as much as he can. If the person is a perfectionist, it is more likely he may suffer from an illusion of control.

SELF-DETERMINATION

Self-determination theory (SDT) is a leading theory in human motivation, based on motivational behavioral science. SDT is a broad framework that studies human motivation and personality. SDT articulates a meta-theory for determining motivational studies, which is an objective theory that defines intrinsic and different extrinsic sources of motivation and describes the corresponding roles of intrinsic and types of extrinsic motivation in cognitive and social development and in personal differences. The theory propositions social and cultural factors that ease or undermine people's sense of volition and initiative, related to an individual's well-being and quality of their achievements. Prospects aiding the individual's experience of autonomy, competence, and relatedness fosters the most volitional and high-quality forms of motivation and engagement for activities, including enhanced performance, persistence, and creativity. Furthermore, SDT proposes that the degree to which any of these three psychological needs are not supported within a social concept will have a robust detrimental impact on wellness in those surroundings.

Motivation, or the "energetic forces that initiate work-related behavior and determine its form, direction, intensity and duration" (Pinder, 2008: 11), is a critical issue for organizations and employees. Motivation links increased employee productivity and organizational revenue, as well as employees' well-being and thriving (Steers, Mowday, & Shapiro, 2004). Given its important role, a good deal of research focuses on the type and extent of motivation employees experience (e.g., Diefendorff & Chandler, 2011; Latham & Pinder, 2005).

We are complex beings who are rarely driven by only one type of motivation. Different goals, desires, and ideas tell us what we want and need. Thus, it is useful to think of motivation on a continuum ranging from "non-self-determined to self-determined" (C. Ackerman, 2018).

Contemporary research proposes alternate needs, such as the need for status (Hogan, 1998) and the need for relatedness (Baumeister & Leary, 1995; Deci & Ryan, 2000). Research on needs as self-determination theory (SDT; Deci & Ryan, 2000) argues that humans are optimally motivated and experience well-being when they have three basic psychological needs satisfied: the need for autonomy, the need for competence, and the need for relatedness (Deci & Ryan). Basic psychological needs have been the focus of research in many domains, such as education (Vansteenkiste, Lens, & Deci, 2006), health care (Ng et al., 2012), sports and exercise (Edmunds, Ntoumanis, & Duda, 2006). Within the domain of organizational research, basic psychological needs have been used across a variety of topics, including leadership (Lian, Ferris, & Brown, 2012), organizational politics (Rosen, Ferris, Brown, Chen, & Yan, 2014), employee well-being (Deci, Ryan, Gagné, Leone, Usunov, & Kornazheva, 2001), person-environment fit (Greguras & Diefendorff, 2009), job design (Van den Broeck, Vansteenkiste, De Witte, & Lens, 2008), and proactive personality (Greguras & Diefendorff, 2010), among others.

SDT is an organismic dialectical approach, which starts under the assumption that people are active organisms, with an evolved inclination toward growing, mastering surrounding obstacles, and implementing the new experiences into a stable sense of self. The natural developmental tendencies are not operating automatically, but instead require ongoing social context, that can either support or thwart the natural tendencies toward activity and psychological growth.

Features for healthy development and functioning related to the concept of basic psychological needs for autonomy, competence, and relatedness. Until the needs are continually satisfied people are happy and experience wellness, in contrast, if the needs are hindered people are not functioning optimally and they feel unhappy. In behavioral science, various types of psychopathology conditions study relate to reactions to basic needs that are hindered.

Formally, SDT encompasses six mini-theories, each developed to describe different motivational based phenomena originated from laboratory and field research. Each of the SDT mini-theories addresses one aspect of motivation or personality functioning, as follows:

1. Cognitive Evaluation Theory (CET) establishes intrinsic motivation, based on the satisfaction of acting "for its own sake." Examples of intrinsic motivation are children playing games and questioning everything, but intrinsic motivation is also a lifelong creative inspiration.

2. Organismic Integration Theory (OIT), explores the topic of extrinsic motivation in its different forms, their features, determinants, and repercussions. OIT is concerned with social concepts that enhance or forestall internalization, or what contributes toward people either resisting, partly adjusting, or deeply internalizing values, goals, or beliefs.

3. Causality Orientations Theory (COT), is the third mini-theory, that addresses personal differences in people's tendencies to adjust toward environments and improve their behavior in multiple ways. This mini-theory explores three types of causality orientations: the autonomy orientation where people act out of self-interest in valuing what is happening; the control orientation in which the focus is on prizes, gains, and approval; and the impersonal orientation which describes anxiety about compe-

tence.

4. The fourth mini-theory is known as Basic Psychological Needs Theory (BPNT) it describes the concept of evolved psychological needs and their relations to psychological well-being. BPNT argues that psychological well-being and functioning depends on autonomy, competence, and relatedness. Thus, concepts that support the hindrance of needs will influence wellness.

5. Goal Contents Theory (GCT), is the fifth mini-theory that arises from the distinctions between intrinsic and extrinsic objectives and their influence on motivation and wellness. Goals partially allow basic need satisfactions and are hence differentially related to well-being. Extrinsic goals are a financial success, appearance, popularity, and fame. Intrinsic goals are a community, personal relationships, and personal development and growth.

6. Relationships Motivation Theory (RMT), is the sixth mini-theory, that explores close relationships, and depicts that interactions are not only desirable for most people but are basic for personal adjustment and well-being because the relationships give the satisfaction of the need for relatedness. Research determinate that not only are the relatedness needs fulfilling in relationships of good quality, but the autonomy need and to some extent the competence need are also fulfilled. According to this mini-theory personal relationships of greatest quality are those where partners support each other and respect each partner's autonomy, competence, and relatedness needs.

SELF-DISCIPLINE

People are confident they can improve their lives if only they had greater willpower. The results of a survey by the American Psychological Association determinate that willpower is the fundamental reason people are not following through with their aims.

Thus it is not surprising psychological scientists have researched willpower for a long time. Especially, trying to determinate who has discipline and under what conditions.

One of the prevailing theories of willpower is known as the energy model of self-control. According to this model, the brain is like a muscle, with a restricted amount of strength, that deplete through exertion. Nobody has discipline all the time; we all have lapsed. And according to the energy model, these lapses happen when one-act out of self-control, which weakens our resolve, leaving us "fatigued" as we turn to another challenge. Various studies have demonstrated that an act of mental exertion can compromise later acts of discipline. Proponents of this theory have reported evidence that the brain—again like a muscle—is fuelled mainly by simple carbohydrates, like sugar, and that reduced willpower is refreshed simply by refueling (J. Leigh, 2012).

"In the long history of humankind (and animal kind, too) those who learned to collaborate and improvise most effectively have prevailed."

Charles Darwin

Other than ability, traits related to determination, such as grit and self-discipline, associate with adaptive outcomes. Different studies have examined the independent effects of these traits on outcomes and the mechanisms involved.

In reality, we face different attitudes related to our everyday activities, due to the fact that people differ from each other. Encountering with difficulties, some people overcome them, others – give up.

Two big boosters of success are self-discipline and motivation. Self-discipline is "the ability to make yourself do things you know you should do even when you do not want to" (Cambridge Dictionaries Online, 2016), "the ability to control one's feelings and overcome one's weaknesses" (Oxford Dictionaries, 2016). It accentuates that "self-discipline appears in various forms, such as perseverance, restraint, endurance, thinking before acting, finishing what you start doing, and has the ability to carry out one's decisions and plans, in spite of inconvenience, hardships or obstacles. Self-discipline also means self-control, the ability to avoid unhealthy excess of anything that could lead to negative consequences" (Sasson, 2016).

A small level of personal self-discipline (or self-control as an arrangement of self-discipline) leads to different problems in social and personal life (Duckworth & Seligman, 2005). However, strong confidence and high level of self-discipline facilitates success, better achievements and achieving the goals (de Ridder, Lensvelt-Mulders, Finkenauer, Stok, & Baumeister, 2012) which, then improve the state of mind and makes people happier and contented (Hofmann, Luhmann, Fisher, Vohs, & Baumeister, 2013). People possessing a high level of self-discipline are better able to control their day-to-day and routine activities, consistently avoid problems, endure with their assignments and surmount hardship. This people always try to find the ideal solution to solve a problem, and they resist desire in unfavorable conditions, which remains longer than those without self-control (Hofmann, Baumeister, Förster, & Vohs, 2012).

Stress in America survey concludes that 27 percent of adults have not adequate self-discipline to improve their lives and make decisive changes in a healthy lifestyle (American Psychological Association, 2011).

Motivation is a crucial component to enhance advancements. However, motivation and self-discipline are not the same. In a simplified manner, we may put equality sign between self-discipline, self-control, self-management and on the other side motivation and inspiration. Motivation has a goal to activate our feelings, to do a thing in which we have an interest. Misconceptions, regularly maintain motivation on a high level, but one day it can be broken into pieces. One must improve motivation constantly to achieve his objectives and accomplish a dream. Hindrance may crush one's illusion when the way to success establishes motivation only. And as a result, one's aims might not be achieved (A. Gorbunovsa, A. Kapenieksb, S. Cakulac, 2016).

In contrast, self-discipline does not depend on emotions. Of course self-discipline is not very popular among people. Self-discipline is a complex and demanding way to achieve success compared to the motivational approach. Truth is self-discipline is the most decisive way of achieving success in life.

There are many self-discipline strategies that work:

1. Stay focused on one thing at a time;

2. Ignore the distractions to cultivate strong self-discipline;

3. Stop multitasking (doing many things at the same time);

4. Train self-discipline (start small, progress from there);

5. Never give up on your aims that take discipline to achieve;

6. Meditate to gain greater focus;

7. Plan ahead;

8. Stay calm;

9. Practice your self-discipline eating healthy food;

10. Practice your self-discipline while exercising;

11. Switch watching the news for comedy shows;

12. Do the toughest chores in the morning;

13. On days when you need your self-discipline the most, consume sugar, because it fuels the brain;

14. Don't make important decisions when starving;

15. Remember why you are doing the staff requiring self-discipline;

16. Do it today;

17. Forgive yourself, plan, and start again.

COMPETENCE

According to the dictionary of American Psychological Association, the word competence is defined as:

1. The ability to exert control over one's life, to cope with specific problems effectively, and to make changes to one's behavior and one's environment, as opposed to the mere ability to adjust or adapt to circumstances as they are. Affirming, strengthening, or achieving a client's competence is often a basic goal in psychotherapy.

2. Competence is one's developed a repertoire of skills, especially as it is applied to a task or set of tasks. A distinction is sometimes made between competence and performance, which is the extent to which competence is realized in one's actual work on a problem or set of problems.

3. In linguistics and psycholinguistics, competence is the nonconscious knowledge of the underlying rules of a language that enables individuals to speak and understand it. In this sense, competence is a rationalist concept that must be kept distinct from the actual linguistic performance of any particular speaker, which may be constrained by such nonlinguistic factors as memory, attention, or fatigue. Both terms were introduced by Noam Chomsky, who proposed the study of linguistic competence as the true task of linguistics; in doing so, he effectively de-

clared linguistics to be a branch of cognitive psychology.

4. In law, competence is the capacity to comprehend the nature of a transaction and to assume legal responsibility for one's actions.

Some authors treat competence as a socially situated concept— the ability to perform tasks and roles to the expected standard —leaving its precise meaning to be negotiated by stakeholders in a macro-or micro-political context. Others treat competence as individually situated, a personal capability or characteristic. This latter concept is labeled 'capability' and it's related to socially-defined competence. It is important to practice representations of competence and for professional preparation of models of the capability to be done (M. Eraut, 2009).

Competencies are defined as "a measurable pattern of knowledge, skill, abilities, behaviors, and other characteristics that each need to have so one can do work roles or occupational functions successfully" (Rodriguez et al., 2002, p. 310). Hence, competencies determinate what people need to do and the behaviors they should undertake for specific activities, tasks or roles to do their professional responsibilities effectively (Schippmann et al., 2000). Competencies are regularly combinations of the knowledge, skills, and abilities necessary to perform a given role (Campion et al., 2011). Practically, various competencies often overlap and cannot be acquired or attained efficiently in a precise manner.

Prahlad and Hamel (1990) were the first to present the concept of determining core competencies. Various scientists have later proposed multiple combinations of core competencies for psychology (e.g., Rodolfa et al., 2005; Fouad et al., 2009); however, no unified set of core competencies exists.

A competency model is a groundwork for defining the skills and knowledge criteria of an occupation. It represents a collection of requisite skills, and their combination jointly defines successful job performance (Baczyriska, 2016). A model extends the concept of a list of competencies and it defines how the individual competencies relate among each other. An organizational psychologist first introduced the term competency modeling in the mid-1970s (McClelland, 1973). Therefore, organizations have used competency-based methodologies and approaches for many years.

Over the last 40 years, competency modeling and the use of competencies to explain the characteristics necessary for effective performance have become increasingly popular (Dai and Liang, 2012; Sliter, 2015).

THE ART OF MANIPULATION

"There are those whose primary ability is to spin wheels of manipulation. It is their second skin and without these spinning wheels, they simply do not know how to function." (C. JoyBell C.)

Psychological manipulation is the exercise of undue influence through mental distortion and emotional exploitation, with the intention to take power, control, benefits, and privileges at the victim's expense (M.B.S.A. Ni, 2014).

The manipulator intentionally creates an imbalance of power and exploits the victim to aid his or her agenda.

Most manipulative people have four common characteristics:

1. They recognize how to detect your weaknesses.

2. Once determinate, they manipulators use your weaknesses against you.

3. Through their astute machinations, they prompt you to give up something of yourself so it may serve their self-centered intentions.

4. In work, social, and family situations, once a manipulator prospers in taking advantage of you, he or she will likely repeat the

violation until you put a stop to the exploitation. (M.B.S.A. Ni, 2014).

For instance: Jessica intends to do A, but Oliver wishes her to do B instead. Oliver has tried unsuccessfully to offer Jessica reasons why she should do B and not A. Oliver might deploy any of the following tactics to try to change Jessica's decision. He might:

1. Oliver can use his appeal on Jessica to persuade her to please him by doing B.

2. Overstate the benefits of doing B and the difficulties of doing A, and/or understate the difficulties of doing B and the benefits of doing A.

3. Blame Jessica and make her feel guilty for favoring to do A.

4. Drag Jessica into an emotional state that makes doing B seems more suitable than it actually is.

5. Explain that doing A will make Jessica seem less admirable and attractive to her acquaintances.

6. Cause Jessica into feeling bad about the situation and characterize A as a decision that will confirm or heighten this feeling, and/or characterize B as a decision that will disprove or fight it.

7. Do tiny favor for Jessica before requesting her to do B, so that she feels in some way compelled to obey.

8. Influence Jessica into hesitation about her own judgment so that she will rely on Oliver's recommendation to do B.

9. Explain with certainty to Jessica that if she decides to do A and not B, Oliver will pull back from their friendship, mope, or become annoyed and generally unpleasant with Jessica.

10. Centre Jessica's attention on some feature of doing A that she is anxious about and ramp up that concern to get her to change her decision about doing A.

The above-explained strategies except for being commonplace in ordinary life are also a form of psychological manipulation. Whether the strategy seems manipulative may depend on different factors and conditions.

Manipulation is generally described as a form of influence that is neither intimidation nor rational persuasion. Therefore, the term "manipulation" usually refers to profound programming or reprogramming of all or most of a person's beliefs, desires, and other mental states.

Psychological manipulation if successful completely deprives its victim of free will actions and freedom, however, common forms of manipulation do the same, but on a more restricted scale. Manipulation is often pronounced to "bypass", "undermine", or "subvert" the target person rational deliberation.

Plenty of philosophical attention in business ethics concentrates on whether advertising is a manipulative process. The economist John Kenneth Galbraith famously characterized advertising as "the manipulation of consumer desire" and compared being the target of advertising with being attacked by demons which inspired in him a passion sometimes for silk shirts, sometimes for kitchenware, sometimes for chamber pots, and sometimes for orange squash (Galbraith 1958).

Various other philosophers also made criticisms of advertising. Generally, these criticisms are referring to advertising that does not clearly convey accurate credible information.

An early example of trickery based approach to manipulation is found in a 1980 paper by Vance Kasten, who explains that manipulation occurs when there is a difference in kind between what one intends to do and what one actually does, when that difference is identifiable to another in a specific way the victim is misled (Kasten 1980: 54).

There are certain norms or ideals that govern beliefs, desires, and emotions. Manipulative action is the undertaking to get someone's beliefs, desires, or emotions to disregard these norms, and to fall short of these ideals (Noggle 1996: 44).

According to Anne Barnhill manipulation is precisely influencing someone's beliefs, desires, or emotions such that she falls short of ideals for belief, desire, or emotion in ways generally not in her self-interest or likely not in her self-interest in the existing context. (Barnhill, 2014).

Claudia Mills proposes a theory related to the trickery account: We might say, then, that manipulation in some way is offering good reasons, when in fact it does not. A manipulator attempts to change individual's beliefs and desires by offering her faulty reasoning, camouflaged as good, or faulty arguments, disguised as sane—where the manipulator himself knows these are atrocious reasons and bad arguments (Mills 1995:100; see Benn 1967 and Gorin 2014b).

Jason Hanna thinks that we should define manipulation as an attempt to propose an objectively defective mental state into the target person's deliberations (Hanna 2015:634; Sunstein 2016:89). Anne Barnhill defends a trickery account of manipulation but suggests that our usage of the term "manipulation" is conflicting regarding whose standards decide whether the manipulator tries to induce the target person to adopt defective mental state (Barnhill).

The use of pressure is manipulative only if the aspiring manipulator directs it at some alleged weakness of his target that will make the target not to resist it. (Rudinow 1978, Tomlinson 1986; Sher 2011; Mandava & Millum 2013).

The idea that manipulation is wrong because it undermines autonomous choice is in discussions about the manipulation of many philosophers.

The inquiry, what type of intention makes an action to count as manipulative has useful implications for evaluating the behavior of children, who sometimes behave in manners that seem manipulative even though they are too young to have the complex intentions that some theories of manipulation propose.

Similarly, to some people manipulation is a habit or a part of their character.

Certainly, some personality disorders, such as borderline personality disorder and antisocial personality disorder, are regularly described by manipulation, as is the purported Machiavellian personality type (Christie & Geis 1970). Furthermore, psychiatrist Len Bowers concludes the manipulative behavior of some personality-disordered (PD) patients is consistent and frequent. It is an essential part of their interpersonal style, a part of the very disorder itself (Bowers 2003).

Few explanations of manipulation relate its moral status to the fact that it influences behavior by methods similar to how a person might use a tool or a device. Therefore manipulation involves treating the target person as a used device, and not as a rational person. Thus, Claudia Mills concludes, a manipulator interest is in reasons not as logical justifiers but as causal advantages. For the manipulator, reasons are tools, and bad reasons can perform as a good one (Mills 1995: 100–101).

In the above case, a manipulator treats his target, not as a rational person, which would need having good reasons for doing as the manipulator proposes. Instead, the manipulator treats his target as a person whose behavior is evoked by pressing the most effective "causal levers".

Certainly, this idea of treating a person as an object is an immoral and outstanding feature of Kant's account of respect for persons. Hence, Kantian ideas elaborate on the idea that manipulation is wrong because of the way that it treats the target person. Thomas E. Hill writes, the idea that one should try to reason with others and not manipulate them by non-rational techniques is manifest in Kant's discussion of the duty to respect others. (Hill 1980: 96)

These deliberations do not entail that it is hopeless to look at this idea of treating other persons as things for an account of the wrongness of manipulation. But they do imply that manipulation is wrong because it treats the person as a simple thing used at convenience.

SELF-ACTUALIZATION

"Self-actualization" is an idea derived from humanistic psychological theory and, specifically, from the theory created by the American psychologist Abraham Maslow. Self-actualization, according to Maslow, represents the growth of an individual toward fulfillment of the highest needs that represent the meaning of life. Carl Rogers created a theory suggesting a "growth potential" whose aim is to integrate correspondingly the "real self" and the "ideal self" thereby originating emergence of the "fully functioning person." It was Maslow, who created a psychological hierarchy of needs, or fulfillment of which theoretically leads to the culmination of the fulfillment of "being values," or the needs that are on the highest level of this hierarchy, representing meaning (A. Olson, 2013).

Psychologist Abraham Maslow's theory of self-actualization emerged from the humanistic perspective, it determinates that people are highly motivated to fulfill their life potential, particularly the need to actualize themselves.

Self-actualization described by Maslow as the ability to surpass levels of physiological, psychological and social needs, in order to obtain fulfillment of personal needs related to life's meaning. He stated that growth is a linear escalation of fulfillment represented by a pyramidal hierarchy. The levels that Maslow describes represent these needs and their order of hierarchical transcendence. The needs in order of hierarchical ascension are as follows:

1. Physiological needs depicted by hunger, thirst, air and sleep;

2. Safety needs, are the needs for security and protection; (Safety needs become prominent in situations of social or political instability);

3. The needs for belongingness and love; these needs have two forms: (a) The drive to fulfill deficiency-based needs for others in a selfish way represented by taking instead of giving, and (b) The need for non-possessive and generous love based on growth and not deficiency;

4. Self-esteem needs or the needs for self-respect and positive feelings consequent to great respect; and

5. The last stage of self-actualization relates to the "being" needs, indicated by the needs for creative self-development of one's potential toward a goal and a sense of meaning in life (A. Reitan, 2013).

Maslow explained in 1943 that higher needs usually won't be pursued until lower needs are met. However, a need does not have to be completely satisfied for someone to move on the next need in the hierarchy. Therefore, the needs have to be partly satisfied, meaning that a person can pursue all five needs, at least to some extent, at the same time.

Maslow included caveats to explain why some people may pursue higher needs before lower ones. For instance, some people who are compelled by a desire to express themselves creatively, and they may pursue self-actualization even when lower needs are not met.

To him, self-actualization is the ability to be the best version of oneself. Maslow explained, "This tendency might be phrased as the desire to become more and more what one is, to become everything that one is capable of becoming."

People have multiple values, ambitions, aspirations, desires, abilities, and capacities. Thus, self-actualization will manifest differently in different people. One individual may self-actualize through art, while another will do so by becoming a parent, and another by inventing new technologies (C. Vinney, 2018).

In 1976, research done by Wahba and Bridwell determinate that some people are more naturally motivated towards self-actualization than others. Those people who can successfully self-actualize, all along achieving moments of joy and transcendence are called self-actualizers.

LUCIFERIANISM

Christians generally acknowledge Satan and Lucifer as two names of the same entity. Worshipers of Satan regularly use these terms interchangeably. Luciferians, believe Satan and Lucifer are separate entity so does the Bible.

Luciferianism is a belief system that worships and respects the attributes and features represented by Lucifer as exhibited in novels and in the Hebrew Bible.

Even though Luciferianism is regularly confused with Satanism because, in a mistaken translation of the bible from Latin, description of Satan is as a fallen Lucifer. However, Luciferians do not admire Satan, rather model themselves after the original Lucifer, who is characterized by sophistication, enlightenment, wisdom, and progressiveness.

Lucifer means creativity, freedom, perfection, development, achievement, exploration, and knowledge through experience over acknowledged truths. He represents rebellion from dogma and other aspects of control.

Some people believe Lucifer and Satan are two sides of the same coin. The perception depends upon personal spiritual goals and understanding. Satan is the more rebellious and adversarial figure. Luciferians see Satanists as primarily resisting something (Christianity specifically and dogmatic religion in general) while Luciferians walk their own path separate from religion.

Luciferians describe this concept as saying that it is all about perspective. People believe that while Lucifer and Satan are the same beings, according to Luciferian he is not Satan because his name means 'the enemy.' This is "Satan" in its original, Hebraic meaning. Satan originally wasn't a name but a description. He was the adversary, challenging the Hebrews to lose faith (C. Beyer, 2019).

Balance is an important constituent of the concept of Lucifer. He is both divine and earthly entity, however, this doesn't matter since the focus is on the principles. Lucifer is both light and darkness since one can not exist without the other.

According to K. Beyer (2018), Luciferians try not to idealize Lucifer but generally seek enlightened knowledge. Their perception of Lucifer is different from the traditional Christian view where they mistakenly confuse Lucifer with Satan. The practitioners are not dependent on the celestial being, they appreciate the opportunity to follow the doctrine of Lucifer, that allows them freedom in their actions and will, although always calculated about the possible repercussions and gains from their undertakings. The confident social concepts or stigma can not hinder one from achieving their destiny. However poor decisions are not an option. A Luciferian is superior and determined to seek wealth and success, all along taking pride in his actions and of himself.

Luciferians believe they should never be disregarded or underestimated to benefit others. According to them, instinctive natural impulses are not sinful.

When a Luciferian faces a cruel person they treat the same with reciprocity. He is kind to others, but his pride doesn't allow him to treat others better than they deserve.

The small numbers of faithful followers of Luciferianism add to the exclusivity of the élite group. Self-determination, self-discipline, self-awareness, self-actualization, and self-motivation are psychological phenomena common among this elitist group. Luciferians protect the environment, support knowledge, science, and art.

Fate depends only on the Luciferian, obstacles are its components, and overcoming them is their obligation. Happiness and unhappiness depend only on the person. The practitioner doubts all things, hence he acquires knowledge.

The name of the Pentagram derives from the Greek "pente", or five, and "gramma", or a letter. The upright pentagram is representing the Morning Star, Christ or the spirit of Lucifer depicted by the divine over the physical. The pentagram is a powerful symbol that represents a balance of five different components of the divine creation: spirit, air, fire, water, and earth.

One position of the upright pentagram directs towards the spirit pointing up, it is a sign of Christ the prime creator or Christ alike the illuminated divine. Alternatively, the up position of this pentagram depicts the human head and knowledge. Furthermore, gnostic scholars worship this pentagram symbol under the phrase Solomon's seal.

Eliphas Levi states The star of the microcosm, or the magic Pentagram, that star wherein the human figure sketched by Agrippa, with the head in the ascending point and the four members in the four other points.

Kabalists name for upright pentagram is its Latin translation Pentaculnm Salomonis. Occultist believes that an upright pentagram has all-powerful virtues since it revolves around the three divine triangles that represent the mighty Trinity.

According to Éliphas Lévi: the inverted pentagram, with two points in the ascendant, in contrast, represents Satan, and the goat of the Sabbath.

The inverted or upside-down pentagram is symbol worshiped by followers of the Left-Hand Path and Satanists. This is the pentagram with two points in the ascendant position, or pointed down which represents the spirit to the governance of matter. This means that the desires of the flesh are before that of the divine spirit and soul. The inverted pentagram reverses our true nature to drain the life energy from our souls (Moe, 2013).

On this subject Aleister Crowley taught "Do what thou will shall be whole of the Law".

The followers of the church of Satan believe that he depicts: indulgence, vitality, wisdom, selective kindness, revenge, selective responsibility, sinful behavior, and the church.

CONCLUDING REMARKS

In religion, the sin of pride is the sin of sins. It was this sin, we're told, that supposedly transformed Lucifer in adversary to God, the "seal of perfection, full of wisdom and perfect in beauty," (Ezekiel, 28:12) into Satan, the devil, the father of lies, the one for whom Hell itself was created (John 8:44, Matthew 25:41). We're warned to guard our hearts against pride lest we too "fall into the same condemnation as the devil" (Timothy 3:6).

It was the sin of pride which first led Eve to eat of the forbidden fruit. Written in Genesis is: "Then the serpent said to the woman, 'You will not surely die. For God knows that in the day you eat of it, your eyes open, and you will be like God, knowing good and evil.' So when the woman saw that the tree was good for food, that it was pleasant to the eyes, and a tree desirable to make one wise, she took of its fruit and ate. She also gave to her husband with her, and he ate" (Genesis, 3:4-6). The serpent who first introduced Eve to this sin of pride was none other than the devil himself (Revelation 12:9, 20:2).

Eager to share his condemnation with others St. Augustine of Hippo (354-430 A.D.) wrote, "Pride is the commencement of all sin" (Ecclesiasticus 10:12-13).

It the overthrew of the devil, that arose the origin of sin, and when his malice and envy pursued man, who was yet standing in his uprightness, it subverted him in the same way in which he fell. For the serpent, in fact, only sought for the door of pride whereby to enter when he said, 'Ye shall be as gods.'"(Philip Schaff)

Pride is a preoccupation with self. Pride revolves around "me, myself, and I." Satan's animosity towards God began with "I". And so it all starts with us. If one's preoccupation is oneself, one is suffering from the sin of pride.

Psychology is not a precise science, to get to the truth we some times must set aside our certainties and look from a different angle. However, some truths are so close and distinct to the mind that man needs just to open his eyes to see them. A person awareness that he posses a self-governing consciousness will grow above the uninvolved acknowledgment of truths. Especially since knowledge has value as it contributes to the development of the person. Certainly, knowledge through facts develops an awareness of the world. However, it seems many people are living dissatisfied lives. It is actually the thirst for knowledge that rises most of this dissatisfaction.

The sad truth in today's materialism based world is that compulsion is what primarily leads society. It is up to us to start a change in our thinking to make passion the motivating power behind our decisions. Not allowing a chance to lead our life and following our passion is a sure way to achieving success and happiness. However, it is our habits and subjective thinking that forbid us to live our life to the fullest. It is the personal wish to succeed that must take precedence.

The human learns their behavior, hence all behavior may be unlearned and new manners of conducting oneself may be learned in its place. If you acquire a habit of constantly following your passion, external diversions will not hamper you on your way to the new you, who is the one following his heart's wish. This new you is somewhat different from your usual self because this new you is achiever who has his personal priorities in order. What those priorities are, is for you to decide, since you are the one for whom your obligation is to do your best, because you are what you make of yourself.

In reality, it is quite possible for one to receive a rejection, most often than not this rejection is in the romance department, but it is not always the case. Here is the hearty monologue "I am not important, only because you don't want me" or vice versa "I am important because you want me". However, not a monologue, but a sentence you should tell to yourself is "I am important because I love and appreciate myself". Subsequently, this rejection of the one you love most, yourself must lead you to take offense against the second party. It is only out of respect for yourself that you need to keep a distance from the second party who hurt you with their rejection. It will probably hurt for a long time, it may hurt for even your lifetime, but dignity is not something that you can compromise with.

The truth is if you fall once you will always fall, and it relates to professional and personal life as well.

When it comes to social anxiety, one must never accept and trust things about himself that other people tell him. Rather It is essential to ask, "Is this realistic?". When someone tells you something important ask yourself is this really true, and don't accept it at face value, just because someone said it. This will open to you entirely new ways of thinking and perceiving reality, both in the seen and unseen realm, from which everything else will appear. You must know that for a matrix of revolutionary beliefs to arise, a subjective movement must originate them in revolt and out of hope.

Nowadays it is quite easy to conclude that there's a shortage of morality in the world. Most of the people today are not motivated to behave ethically, and morality is not prominent in their thinking.

I believe the greatest moral challenge of our time is our flawed concept of morality. Our inclinations when we think and talk about morality prevents our ability to engage with views other than our own, it makes managing diversity and disagreement harder and is inclined to lock us into thinking patterns that produce more instances of adversity and unrest than they can solve. (T. Dean, 2018)

In contemporary societies, people all over the world face an analogous set of social problems and use an analogous set of moral rules to solve them. Certainly, different societies have a different framework of moral rules.

In my opinion, today's world and morality, are an oxymoron, because people today are hardly interested in the greater good. There are very little rules about what is right, which has profound consequences in societies.

This level of moral collapse should not surprise anyone, especially since, after performing immoral deeds, people are saying: "So what? What is the big deal?"

Moral systems are structures for cooperation, they are giving us reasons, approaches, and responsibilities related to inter-personal cooperation. A predominant social system in the world today is capitalism, which directs people that they have an imperative to compete with everyone. This means the only guideline is cunning, ruthless and an immoral one, to compete against each other, for personal gain!

A lot of people life's are hardly likely to change despite their persistent actions. This is because no one is open to cooperate, rather compete with, leading the poor people on the edge of the unwanted direction they had taken upon themselves to live through. Not surprisingly, many people who rise their status in today's society have little if any moral values, or respect for the moral norms and rules.

This leads me to my last question "Is rejecting morality the price one must pay so he can succeed today?"

When it comes to the moral degeneration of Lucifer through his pride, in contrast to today's values his breach of moral ethics was a minor one. Upbringing today emphasizes Lucifer's sin-pride as desired psychological feature, which was what created the snowflake generation.

Currently, there is new morality taking over the world stage. It has concepts like self-fulfillment, living the best possible life, being your ideal self. Traditional morality is in clear downfall, because of this reason a person must adapt to the changes taking place so he can follow the world that is fast-forwarding.